Grea
Special Events

And Activities!

By Morton, Prosser and Spangler

Venture Publishing, Inc.
State College, PA

Cover Design: Annie Morton and Julie Turner

Library of Congress Catalogue Card Number 91-65991
ISBN 0-910251-45-2

In token payment for patience and understanding
this book is dedicated to
Kiely Morton and Cathy Frazier
with affection and appreciation
and
Paul Ellis
for inspiration and leadership.

GREAT SPECIAL EVENTS AND ACTIVITIES

TABLE OF CONTENTS

Introduction

Celebrate What Is.....Festivals _ _ _ _ _ _ _ _ _ _ _ _ _ 1-15

Wet & Wild.....Aquatics _ _ _ _ _ _ _ _ _ _ _ _ _ 16 - 20

Romper Stompers.....Pre-School _ _ _ _ _ _ _ _ _ _ _ 21 - 24

Kids Korner.....Youth _ _ _ _ _ _ _ _ _ _ _ _ _ _ 25 - 37

Too Kool To Recreate.....Teens _ _ _ _ _ _ _ _ _ _ _ 38 - 43

Yuppies and Up.....Adults _ _ _ _ _ _ _ _ _ _ _ _ 44 - 49

Off The Rocker.....Seniors _ _ _ _ _ _ _ _ _ _ _ _ 50 - 55

The Whole Gang.....Family _ _ _ _ _ _ _ _ _ _ _ 56 - 64

Ah Outdoors......Nature _ _ _ _ _ _ _ _ _ _ _ _ 65 - 70

Socks and Jocks.....Sports _ _ _ _ _ _ _ _ _ _ _ 71 - 80

Beat Feet.....Road Races _ _ _ _ _ _ _ _ _ _ _ _ 81 - 86

Tis The Season.....Holidays _ _ _ _ _ _ _ _ _ _ _ 87 - 99

Do if You Dare....??? _ _ _ _ _ _ _ _ _ _ _ _ _ 100 - 101

Recreators Tool Box _ _ _ _ _ _ _ _ _ _ _ _ _ 102 - 112

INTRODUCTION

Fun is contagious...and limitless in its forms of expression. But it has to start somewhere. Fun is generated by people who put their great ideas to work so others can play.

GREAT SPECIAL EVENTS AND ACTIVITIES is a collection of ideas from professionals in the areas of recreation, cultural arts and shopping malls. This book can be utilized by anyone who wants to contribute to the quality of life of those around them. This "idea book" encourages you to make your own additions, deletions and adaptations. After all, you know your resources better than anyone. Although GREAT SPECIAL EVENTS AND ACTIVITIES is divided into age and event categories, most events and activities can be enjoyed by any age, in some way, shape or fun. The Earthworm Race, for example, is included in the chapter for youths, but can be played by adults, as well.

HOW TO USE THIS BOOK

Our suggestion is this: Use your imagination and adapt, adapt, adapt. Use two or three events and produce a new event that you can call your own — then send it to us for our second book! (See the form in the back of the book.) Many of the ideas in GREAT SPECIAL EVENTS AND ACTIVITIES are those of the authors, but a larger portion of the ideas come from other creative people. Whether it was a one on one conversation, material received in a conference setting, or something we read, we collected the information for the use of other leisure programmers. In particular, we would like to express our thanks to the following people and agencies to for their contributions: Jan Bankhead, Bob Valenti, Fort Mill Recreation Department, Virginia Beach Recreation Department, the City of Greenville Parks and Recreation Departments, and Jackson Recreation and Parks Departments.

Appreciation, also, to friends who assisted in the production of GREAT SPECIAL EVENTS AND ACTIVITIES: Doug Becker, Cathy Frazier, Julie Kallam Turner, Lynne Lucas, James Pulley, Cindy Tucci and Megan Ferree.

Thanks to each and everyone of you who made GREAT SPECIAL EVENTS AND ACTIVITIES possible by contributing an idea or event. We hope we have not excluded any credits for event ideas that were submitted for the sole purpose of this book, and apologize if we inadvertently omitted your name.

ABOUT THE AUTHORS

Annie Morton is currently Membership Coordinator for The LifeCenter, a health and conditioning club in Greenville, South Carolina. Her heart is still very much in the field of recreation, where she served the profession for seven years. GREAT SPECIAL EVENTS AND ACTIVITIES is her brain child and many of the events within these pages are Annie's creations. Annie has two children — Todd and Kiely — who are both students at Florida State University. Annie resides in Greenville, South Carolina and in her spare time likes to camp, hike and bike in the mountains.

Angie Prosser, a 1985 graduate from Clemson University, began her career at the City of Greenville Parks and Recreation Departments in Greenville, South Carolina, where she is currently the Special Events Supervisor. Despite the fact that Angie volunteered her time on the book two years after its conception, she became the driving force behind its organization and completion. Without Angie's computer abilities desktop publishing skills, and perserverance, GREAT SPECIAL EVENTS AND ACTIVITIES would still be hand written on legal pads. When Angie isn't working on the weekends, she enjoys camping with friends and "The Dooder" — her black toy poodle.

Sue Spangler recently moved from Illinois to Charlotte, North Carolina, where she is Recreation Superintendent for the City of Charlotte. Sue is best known for promoting and encouraging "Off the Wall" events. Many of these innovative ideas that Sue has collected at speaking engagements help comprise GREAT SPECIAL EVENTS AND ACTIVITIES. Sue has been quoted as saying "Isn't it fun to have fun?" and practices what she believes!

CELEBRATE
WHAT IS....

FESTIVALS

PASSPORT TO RECREATION
(OR PASSPORT TO FITNESS OR PASSPORT TO CULTURE)

DESCRIPTION:

Participants can enter into a new world using their Passport to Recreation. Enthusiastic "travelers" will be awarded when they complete different levels of participation within a certain time period. The passport is a small 10 to 12 page book, (4 1/2" x 5 1/2") with each page defining 3 or 4 qualifying events/activities (see next page) and upon completion, a staff person at each participating facility stamps the appropriate block. Tie in passport events and activities with themes, days and programs already established by your

community and recreation department. Try to make all events free and /or offer enough alternatives so the activities requiring admission could be eliminated and the participant could still qualify for awards; or arrange free admisssion or discount admissions to passport holders. Upon completion of the passport book, the participant takes the book to the nearest recreation center to be entered into the appropriate prize level drawing. Qualifying activities/events could include: hike a trail; visit the zoo; ride with the ranger; enroll in an instructional class; participate in a sports clinic (event); swim laps; pick up a leisure guide from a recreation center; stop by the AARP to pick up literature; visit the art museum; go to a city league softball game; write a paragraph about an ultimate recreation experience; bring in a photo of you and your family having fun; paddle in a paddle boat; play a game of tennis, golf, basketball; attend a recreation department special event; color a recreation department coloring contest form; bring in a newspaper article that mentions the recreation department.

RELATED ACTIVITIES:

Develop a "Walk Book" containing detailed walking trails, including some walks in the uptown area for uptown employees; plan an event just for women; a flashlight golf tournament; photo contest using photos brought in to collect a stamp; series of Bag Day Concerts (see page 3), "Expose yourself to the Arts" (free art exhibit by area artists).

RESOURCES:

Secure 2 or 3 major sponsors, one of which should be a radio sponsor. Distribution of passports could be through instructional classes at the recreation centers, sporting goods stores, library, sponsors, and places where qualifying events/activities will take place. If a major corporation or bank is the major sponsor of this event, bill it as First Acme's gift to the participant--"for your support and involvement in the opportunities available in the community."

CREATIVE PROMOTIONS:

Prepare cable broadcast of your department's programs and special events. Set up a recreation department exhibit in city hall or in a bank lobby advertising the Passport to Recreation Program.

JUDGING CATEGORIES:

To qualify for incentive prizes and final prizes, three levels of participation should be established: Sampler (Minimum - 5 stamps), Explorer (Minimum - 12 stamps); Master Adventurer (Minimum -16 stamps). Final prize winners are selected at random from all entries received. Incentive prizes are different at each level.

PASSPORT TO RECREATION

YOUR PASSPORT TO RECREATION

The Charlotte Parks and Recreation Department, Coca-Cola, WBCY and Circle K invite you to participate in the "Passport to Recreation" program, another "Life. Be In It." activity.

On the following pages are listed more than 20 Parks and Rec activities. During the month of July, National Recreation and Park Month, participate in at least ten of these recreation adventures and qualify for prize drawings. The more activities in which you participate, the more valuable prize you are eligible to win.

Listed below are the three prize levels and the number of stamps required to qualify:

- **Red Level** (10 stamps): "Life. Be In It." t-shirts, six packs of Coca-Cola product, Parks and Rec Golf Passes*
- **White Level** (11-15 stamps): Park and Rec Season Swim Passes*, Coca-Cola Coolers
- **Silver Level** (16-20 stamps): Park and Rec Day Camp Passes*, Two Nights Hotel Accommodations at Myrtle Beach

HOW TO PARTICIPATE

1. Go by any Circle K store and pick up your Passport to Recreation. Each participant must have their own Passport and should complete the identification section accordingly.

2. Throughout the month of July, participate in the designated recreation adventures during the identified time schedules.** Prior to leaving the facility/event, have a recreation staff member place a stamp in the square beside the appropriate activity in the

Passport. All stamps located in the Passport must be from the Charlotte Parks and Recreation Department.

3. Once you have received the required number of stamps for your desired prize level, take your Passport to the nearest recreation center or mail it to: Charlotte Parks and Recreation Department, 1900 Park Drive, Charlotte, NC 28204. Your name will then be entered in the appropriate prize level drawing. Winners will be selected at random from all entries received.

4. Employees (and their IRS dependents) of Charlotte Parks and Recreation Department, Coca-Cola, WBCY and Circle K stores, their agencies and affiliates are not eligible to participate in drawings. Deadline for all entries is Wednesday, August 6, 1986.

PARTICIPANTS HAVE THE ENTIRE MONTH OF JULY TO PARTICIPATE IN THE PROGRAM

* Charlotte Parks and Recreation passes are only good for calender year 1987.
** Some of the Passport adventures are only held on specific days and/or times.

Name _____

Address _____

City/State_____ Zip _____

Phone_____ Age _____

SWIMMING:
Any of our pools provide a refreshing experience.
Cordelia   2100 North Davidson Street
Double Oaks 2600 Statesville Avenue
Greenville   1330 Spring Street
Revolution   1130 Remount Road
Tuesday-Saturday - 10 a.m.-12 p.m.
              1- 7 p.m.
     Sunday - 1- 6 p.m.
     Monday - closed

HORNETS NEST PARK ZOO:
Enjoy a furry friend at our petting zoo.
6301 Beatties Ford Rd. (5 miles North of I-85)
Tuesday-Friday   - 9 a.m.- 2 p.m.
Saturday-Sunday - 9 a.m.- 5 p.m.

GOLF:
Nine challenging holes at Revolution Golf Course at Remount Road and Barringer Drive. Electric and pull carts available.

RECREATION CENTER:
Take a tour of any Rec Center and pick up a program schedule complete with a list of all city centers on the back.

DAY CAMP/PLAYGROUND:
Try out our summer day camps and/or playground programs. Call 336-2884 for sites and times.

CHARLOTTE POPS CONCERT:
Bring a blanket and snacks to Freedom Park and listen to the musicians. July 6, 13, 20th @ 7:15 p.m.

WALKING:
Walk for a minimum of 15 minutes inside or outside any city recreation center.

LIVELY ARTS FESTIVAL:
Enjoy this special arts event July 25 from 11 a.m.-5 p.m. at Independence Park.

SUGGESTED PRIZES:

Incentive Prizes: T-shirts with logo of your department, and all the sponsors' logos; product and/or, coupons from sponsors; promotional items such as coffee mugs, frisbees, miniature footballs, basketballs, posters, bumper stickers. Final prizes: free golf weekend; free aerobic classes for a year; 4 month membership at a fitness center; lunch with a local sports figure or sportscaster; tennis match with a pro; season tickets to AA baseball; gift certificate from a local sporting goods store.

City of Charlotte Parks and Recreation Departments, 600 East Fourth Street, Charlotte, NC 28202-2864

RED, WHITE, AND BOOM!

Plan a Forth of July festivity to include frisbee golf, inner tube races, water baseball championship, barber shop quartet, anything goes contest, sky divers, cloggers, gold fish chase, penny hunt, musical ice bucket, pinata bust, watermelon cutting.

BAG DAYS CONCERT SERIES

DESCRIPTION:

Set up a series of concerts in a park or mall area where it is convenient for workers to eat their lunch and enjoy free entertainment. Contract with local artists and entertainers to perform during lunchtime. (Offer small fee --$100.00-- or ask for free performance). The performers benefit because they receive free publicity, plus a varied audience that they may attract to their clubs.

RELATED ACTIVITIES:

Ask sandwich shop or lunch merchant to have coupon printed on the bag or flyer.

MATERIALS:

Stage with electricity, chairs or benches for audience, flyers.

POSSIBLE RESOURCES:

"House bands" at local hotels and nightclubs are always looking for additional opportunities for promotions. Radio stations may know of local bands and groups that need the publicity.

CREATIVE PROMOTIONS:

Have schedule of events printed on a brown paper bag; or print schedule or an invitation inviting the public to lunch in the park or mall. Distribute the flyer to all area businesses, corporations and stores in the vicinity of the concert area.

City of Greenville Parks and Recreation Departments, 103 Cleveland Park Drive, Greenville, SC 29601

TOUR THE TOWN

Plan a walking tour of your town and trace the development of commercial architecture from the first movie theatre to the most contemporary office building. Tours of the interior may be permitted at some locations.

GREEK FESTIVAL

As most ethnic groups, the Greeks transmit tradition. A Greek festival focuses on food, but could also include cooking demonstrations, film presentations of Greece and the Mediterranean area, tours of the Greek church, arts and crafts, children's events and traditional Greek dances in colorful costumes. Greek foods include roast lamb, oven-roasted potatoes, chicken riganato, souvlakia (marinated tenderloins), keftedes (meatballs seasoned with Grecian spices), pastichio (macaroni, grated cheese and sauteed ground beef), rice pilaf, fasoulakia (seasoned green beans in tomato sauce), tiropita (pastry filled with mixture of cheeses), spanakopita (pastry layered with spinach and feta cheese), koulourakia (a braided doughnut) kataifi (shredded wheat with honey) and Greek salad.

BLACK ARTS FESTIVAL

DESCRIPTION:

A Black Arts Festival is both enjoyable and educational. Entertainment is the main focus, tapping local, regional and national talent. Areas of entertainment could include: choral and gospel groups, blues groups, jazz ensembles, reggae music, combos, play productions, poetry readings, dance groups, and storytellers. Additional activities such as visual arts, African artifacts, specialized foods, film series, artists in action and arts and crafts sales could be scheduled.

RELATED ACTIVITIES:

An appropriate time, weather permitting, would be during Black History Week. Include black leaders from the community in your opening ceremonies. A big name group could make this a great fund raiser.

MATERIALS:

Staging, sound equipment, display panels and hanging equipment, films or videos, screen, tables, chairs, flyers, posters.

POSSIBLE RESOURCES:

Arts council, art associations, churches, schools, school teachers, state art commission.

CREATIVE PROMOTIONS:

Attractive poster, 30 second radio spots (public service announcements).

JUDGING CATEGORIES:

Prizes for visual arts entries, and Best show 'n' tell, Black History Quiz.

Pat Cadle, Southern Pines Recreation and Parks Departments, Box 870, Southern Pines, NC 28387

HISTORIC BIKE TOUR

DESCRIPTION:

Select some of the outstanding and impressive historical sites in your city or county; establish a scenic route; and you have the beginnings of a wholesome, educational event. Staff at each historic stop provides both an informative presentation of the site and refreshments.

RELATED ACTIVITIES:

The tour need not be limited to bicycles, but available for walkers and runners.

MATERIALS:

Maps, lemonade, cookies, tables, chairs, First Aid Kit.

POSSIBLE RESOURCES:

The local historic association would be appropriate staff at the stops.

CREATIVE PROMOTIONS:

Utilize bike shops, sporting goods stores and bike clubs for distribution of information.

GIANT TWISTER

Sell individual spaces on a 100 foot by 100 foot polyurethane mat. Follow regular Twister Rules. The last person standing (or not completely falling) wins the Grand Prize, which could be the money from the ticket sales.

APPLE FESTIVAL

DESCRIPTION:
Proud of the fact that their county is the 7th largest apple producing county in the United States, Henderson County, NC holds an apple festival for a week. The entire downtown supports the festival by designing their store windows in an apple theme and offering special prices during the Downtown Sidewalk Sale.

ACTIVITIES:

FOOD:
Big Apple Breakfast (sponsored by Lions Club), Apple Baking Contest

ARTS AND CRAFTS:
Apple Photo Contest, Quilt Fest (show), Arts and Crafts Fair, Apple Decorating Contest, Creative Arts Spectacular (German dancers)

SPORTS:
William Tell Archery Tournament, Apple Jack Open Tournament, Walk-For-Hunger, Softball Tournament, Road Race, Bicycle Tour, Horseshoe Pitching Tournament;

CHILDRENS:
Firemen and Kiddie Parade, Kid's Carnival, Children's Dance and Drama Performance, Miniature Golf Tournament

ENTERTAINMENT:
Apple Time Variety Show, Mountain Folk Dance Jamboree, Downtown Music Festival (Band Contest), Street Dance, King Apple Parade

OTHER:
Apple Juice Plant Tour, Curb Market Special Days, Apple Orchard Tour, Gem and Mineral Spectacular, Bridge Tournament.

RESOURCES:
Lions Club, County Extension, Hunger Coalition, Arts Council.

THIN AIR FESTIVAL

Invite the public to one of your larger parks to experience the thrills of a Thin Air Festival. Allow businesses such as hobby shops, kite shops, and toy stores to set up sales and demonstration booths. Make contests or free play available for the following activities: remote control airplanes, darts, kite flying, boomerangs, frisbees, paper airplanes, wingers, yo-yos, hackysacs, and a balloon volleyball marathon. A particularly fun activity for children is a Balloon Sculpture where children (and adults) add long blown-up balloons to a structure that has been started prior to the opening of the festival. Balloons can be added by tying on to an existing balloon or by stuffing a balloon in between other balloons. Include the sale of helium balloons. Invite a juggler and a clown, or a person who makes animals and objects out of balloons. Larger parks can include hot air balloon tethered rides and demonstrations from hang gliders and ultralights.

GET FIT MONTH

DESCRIPTION:

By dedicating a full month to fitness activities, your department can help start a personal, or perhaps family, fitness routine. Begin by soliciting the help of a corporation dedicated to health and wholesome living. (The recreation agencies in Greenville, SC chose D'Lites of America, a healthy fast food chain). Next, write a letter, accompanied by a form and deadline date, to all agencies, organizations and businesses who are concerned with fitness, i.e. hiking clubs, running clubs, YMCA's, YWCA's, fitness centers, health food stores, diet centers. Suggest that they come up with an activity that could be scheduled at least four times, perferably on the same day of each week, during that month. For instance, a bicycle club would schedule a 10-15 mile ride every Saturday morning. All events would be printed on a large calendar produced by the corporate sponsor.

RELATED ACTIVITIES:

Plan a Kick-Off for Get Fit Month where any of the participating agencies could have a table display and handouts. Include free play sports activities (volleyball, tennis) kiddie games, healthy concessions and entertainment.

MATERIALS:

Posters, flyers, calendar, and, depending on whether or not a kick off is incorporated, athletic equipment, tables, chairs, games, prizes, food and beverages.

POSSIBLE RESOURCES:

Health spas, fitness centers, outing clubs and stores, health food stores, diet centers, hospitals.

CREATIVE PROMOTIONS:

Short radio spots acting as teasers 1 month prior could ask "Are you fit?" or "Get fit-free: be listening to WESC for details." Calendars can be tray liners in co-sponsoring restaurant.

City of Greenville Parks and Recreation Departments, 103 Cleveland Park Drive, Greenville, SC 29601

FOREST FESTIVAL

Juried art show; entrants must use wood in art or craft piece.

PEANUT FEST

Includes a peanut butter sculpture contest, cooking contest, and fireworks.

ENGLISH FESTIVAL OR "JOLLY TIME" FESTIVAL

A fun-filled day of English traditions, including Morris and garland dancers, handbell choir, brass rubbings, curiosity shoppe, dance workshops, and an English Pub that serves fish and chips, English pastries, and Scotch eggs.

SECONDS POTTERY SALE

Potters look forward to this event to sell discontinued lines and seconds.

CARROT FESTIVAL

Held during carrot havesting. Includes a carrot cooking contest and tractor pull.

BED RACE

DESCRIPTION:

Here is a wild, zanny, fun-filled event that can involve the entire community. Participation in the bed race is available to local businesses, agencies, organizations and clubs (fee - $50.00 per entry). Beds are pushed by four runners through an obstacle course -- 1/2 mile in length. This event could also be called "Bed Race for Cure" with all proceeds going to the patients of a nursing home, children's hospital, etc. Awards will be presented to first and second place finishers and the best decorated bed. Each team needs to secure 4 runners and 1 rider. These people may be friends, employees, local teenagers, etc. however, all runners and riders must be 16 years of age or older. Encourage the participants to decorate wild and to use the craziest bed available.

Rules and Regulations:
1) There will be 4 runners per team. Runners push the bed from the starting point, through an obstacle course, and to the finish line.
2) Runners must be 16 years of age or older. Runners under 18 must submit a parental release form signed by a parent or legal guardian.
3) All runners must wear track, tennis, or running shoes. No bare feet allowed.
4) At least one runner must remain with the bed at all times.
5) Each sponsor will provide one rider for each bed during competition.
6) The riders must be of opposite sex from the runners.
7) Queens (female riders) must wear sleepwear over a bathing suit.
8) Kings (male riders) must wear sleepwear over a bathing suit.
9) At the obstacle course the participating runners are soley responsible for stopping the bed with no outside assistance.
10) At the finish line, the runners will be assisted by volunteers in stopping, only after the bed has crossed the line.
11) No assistance by non-team members may be provided runners at any time during the race.
12) Beds and/or runners, which in any way impedes the progress of another bed and/or runner, may be disqualified or penalized at the judges discretion.
13) Violations of any rules during the race may result in disqualification at judge's discretion, with final determination belonging to the Race Chairmen only.

ACTIVITIES:

Plan as part of a festival or as an event on its own.

MATERIALS:

Pre-registration forms, stop watches, judging and record sheets, start/finish lines.

RESOURCES:

Local businesses, agencies, organizations and clubs, fraternities, sororities, high school clubs.

CREATIVE PROMOTIONS:

Send letter of intent application to potential sponsors. Encourage participating agencies to challenge other agencies, through newspaper, radio or television advertising.

JUDGING CATEGORIES:

First and second place for best decorated, most unique, most colorful, most elaborate.

VAN GO

Fill a department van with art enthusiasts and visit the homes and studios of artists and craftsmen. Work with your local art association, which can provide the expertise and help conduct the tour(s).

THE CELEBRATION OF BLACK HISTORY MONTH

DESCRIPTION:

To celebrate the contributions that blacks and their culture have made, your department can pull on local resources or contract services that will provide impressive learning tools and exhibitions. Or you might want to use both. Encourage the participation of local black performers and other professionals by scheduling performances, readings, and discussion panels. Include musicians, writers, artists, singers, groups. Have professionals such as a school principal, radio/television personality, minister, dental surgeon, attorney, etc. take five minutes, each, to answer the moderator's questions at a panel discussion called "Story of Success: In Their Own Words." (What early experiences shaped your career? What was your most positive influence? What have major obstacles been? How have civil rights and women's movements affected your careers? What advice do you have for young people today?) A museum or art center is an appropriate setting for the "Black Women Achievements Against the Odds" panel exhibition that can be purchased from the Smithsonian Art Institution Traveling Exhibition Service (panels that feature black women and their accomplishments in medicine, law, arts, and science) and for the "Folk Art and Crafts: The Deep South" exhibit rented from the Center for Southern Folklore. In one of the larger rooms, schedule a week long film series. Suggested Films: "Gravel Springs, Fife and Drums," "Give My Poor Heart Ease: Mississippi Delta Bluesmen," "Hush Hoggies Hush: Tom Johnson's Praying Pigs," "Nellie's Playhouse," "Sermons In Wood," "Leon "Peck" Clark": "Basket Maker," "The Performed Wood," "Fannie Bell Chapman: Gospel Singer." A living museum is actually an event within itself. Select famous blacks from history or the present and get volunteers from the community ot a theater group to portray these people and "come alive" to tell their achievements. Include Dr. George Washington Carver, Mary Bethune, Marion Anderson, Dr. Martin Luther King, Paul Roberson, Madame C.J. Walker. During Black History Month, get the assistance of a special interest group(s) to sponsor and prepare an "American Fruits With African Roots" tasting. The hostesses demonstrate how to prepare foods from the past, such as pluck and plunder stew, cornmeal mush, greenswith cornmeal dumplings, shortenin' bread, molasses pudding and homemade lemonade.

RELATED ACTIVITIES:

Black Greek Sorority and Fraternity Night; "The Black Economy" lecture (given by a professor of economics), Black Heritage Bowl (student teams quizzed on elements of black history; have preliminary competition leading up to finals and offer a scholarship as grand prize); "Issues and Concerns Facing Black College Students" lecture/discussion; Exerpts from "The Meeting of Martin and Malcolm" presented by a drama club (based on the first and only meeting of Martin Luther King.

POSSIBLE RESOURCES:

For assistance: Local college or university lecturers, art center or museum (for space), senior citizens (cooking), special interest groups and theatre groups (Living Museum). Smithsonian Institution Traveling Exhibition Service, Washington, D.C. for "Black Women: Achievements Against the Odds"; Center For Southern Folklore, 1216 Peabody Ave. P.O. Box 4081, Memphis, TN 38104 for "Folk Art and Crafts: The Deep South"; area businesses to sponsor individual panels of exhibits.
For participation: Church groups, Special interest groups, recreation centers, YWCA, YMCA.

CREATIVE PROMOTIONS:

Develop a one page insert that fits into church programs and get cooperation of churches to have it inserted; select an urban contemporary station for a co-sponsor and call in daily with upcoming activities.

Pat Alford, Jackson Recreation and Parks Dept., Civic Center, 400 South Highland, Jackson, TN 38301

CHILDREN'S THEATRE

DESCRIPTION:
A Children's theatre offers a variety of drama experiences to the community. In addition to children's plays performed by both youth and adults, a theatre especially for children lends itself to workshops, drama classes, dance and music classes and performances by artists from the area and throughout the nation. Greenville, SC housed their children's theatre, (Saturday Storefront Theatre), in a vacant store at the mall.

RELATED ACTIVITIES:
Professional clown and mime performances and workshops; puppet shows and workshops; magic shows and workshops; professional children's dance ensembles, storytellers. Drama classes to include: beginner, creative movement, intermediate, stage combat, music/ dance, Shakespeare, make-up, stage design, lighting and sound, costuming.

MATERIALS:
Staging, curtains, lighting and sound equipment, lumber, paint, brushes, seating, props, flyers, posters, reservation forms.

POSSIBLE RESORCES:
Well-established community theatre, mall, arts center, arts council, community theatre actors, technical crew, school drama teachers, performing artists and groups.

CREATIVE PROMOTIONS:
For "Jack and the Beanstalk," display a giant shoe and a sign reading "The Giant is Coming." For "Cinderella," arrange a hunt for the glass slipper, with clues at various department facilities or the stores in the mall. To kick off the upcoming season, have a premiere party at the theatre, offering, free food and beverages and an attractive brochure of the upcoming shows, auditions, and workshops.

City of Greenville Parks and Recreation Departments, 103 Cleveland Park Drive, Greenville, SC 29601

Greenville County Recreation Commission, 500 Roper Mountain Road, Greenville, SC 29615

ANNUAL/INTERNATIONAL TIME LINE

Features crafts people who vend early American traditional crafts, only, such as blacksmiths, tinsmiths, potters, coppersmiths, weavers, candlemakers, wigmakers, gunsmiths.

OLD FASHIONED SATURDAY NIGHT

Features a country western band playing for a street dance, horse and carriage rides around the city and a silver dollar drawing.

INTERNATIONAL NIGHT IN THE PARK

Choose a country or a theme and then plan an evening affair to include appropriate catered food and entertainment. "Steamboat Night," for instance, would consist of southern cooking and a one act Mark Twain play.

RUBBER DUCK REGATTA

DESCRIPTION:

A Rubber Duck Regatta can be held on a river, stream, waterfall or man-made water trough with moving water. Two to three weeks prior to the event, participants buy tickets ($5.00) to purchase their own entry -- a real rubber duck. Tickets are numbered and the day of the event, participant picks up their number and duck with the matching number. Numbers are written on ducks with waterproof ink or a tag is attached to their necks.

ACTIVITIES:

This can be an event on its own or as part of a large festival. Why not run it along with a remote control boat competition and/or demonstration?

MATERIALS:

Ducks, rubber strings, tags, nets, registration forms.

RESOURCES:

This could be a fund raiser for a charitable organization. For prizes, solict hotels for fantasy weekends, and local restaurants for a dinner for two. March of Dimes.

CREATIVE PROMOTIONS:

To encourage event awareness, display one of the rubber ducks at various ticket outlets, along with a colorful poster advertising event.

JUDGING CATEGORIES:

First three ducks to place are awarded prizes. Everyone gets to keep their duck.

HISTORIC HOME TOUR

DESCRIPTION:

Every community has a history to tell. Tell yours by establishing a route of historic homes and sites. Develop a brochure with a map identifying these places and detailing significant historical information. Designate specific times to offer the tour to various groups (i.e. Scout troops, churches, local clubs, convention delegates/spouses.)

RELATED ACTIVITIES:

Offer in conjunction with a major historical event or festival, Volksmarch (see page 74), Van Go (see page 7), Historic Bike Tour (see page 4).

MATERIALS:

Van, brochures, tour guides, refreshments.

POSSIBLE RESOURCES:

Local historic societies, history professors, from local university.

CREATIVE PROMOTIONS:

Promote through your local Convention and Visitors Bureau, library, Chamber of Commerce.

"KUDZU GROWS ON YOU" FESTIVAL

DESCRIPTION:

"There's a reason for everything," they say, and once you sponsor a Kudzu Festival, people just might beleive that Kudzu has its special purpose, too. What an opportune time to demonstrate the usefulness of Kudzu through hands on arts and crafts, arts performances, cooking and, just plain fun. Your department can make some money, also. There is something for everyone to enjoy at a Kudzu Festival...Kudzu hats, Kudzu baskets (bring a pile of kudzu to the festival and learn to make a basket); handmade paper (grind kudzu in a blender, then cook like soup for pulp); print making onto cloth (roll leaf in textile ink and press onto cloth for design; quilt the back). Performances could include kudzu poetry reading, a Kudzu choir, Kudzu dancers (wearing kudzu) who could perform at an opening ceremony and/or during the festival. Have a special area for the Kudzu Kitchen, where folks can get a taste of fried Kudzu leaves, quiche, salad, noodles, and more. Money makers could include the sales of the Kudzu Kitchen Cookbook, stationery, rubber stamps, seeds, buttons, bumper stickers, t- shirts, posters that are hand signed, a book on "how to get rid of kudzu," kudzu necklaces and wind chimes, poetry books, raffle tickets for kudzu quilt.

RELATED ACTIVITIES:

Arts and Crafts booths, face painting, mask making, mural painting, tug of war using Kudzu vine, Kudzu slogan contest, picnic, competition for Kudzu theme song, photograph exhibition and competition featuring shots of Kudzu.

MATERIALS:

Lots of good strong kudzu, booths, cooking facilities, display panels.

RESOURCES:

Parks department to cut an abundance of kudzu; art instructors, performance groups, graphic artists, concession vendors.

CREATIVE PROMOTIONS:

Play up the persistence of kudzu through radio (talking kudzu). Contact core groups whose members would be interested in participating and/or competing in the various areas.

Suzi Richter, New Prospect Craft Center, Knoxville, TN

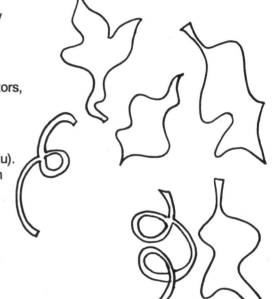

MOBILE ARTS TRUCK

The Arts Truck is a mobile arts studio equipped for workshops and individual activities in printmaking, photography, weaving, and basket making. Professional artists (approved and contracted by the Arts Commission of your state) staff the studio and provide instruction for a four week period. Once your agency has decided to host the Mobile Arts Truck, the Arts Commission sends you a complete packet of all of the requirements you need to host the truck in your area. This includes a week by week checklist, residency costs, site preparation, community coordinator, publicity, scheduling, evaluation, and follow-up assignments. All the publicity is included in the packet; all you have to add is the date, time, location, etc. for the newspaper, radio, and school flyers. The artists send information about themselves. After the four week residency has been completed, judge all photography and silkscreening, and award prizes.

PIONEER DAYS

DESCRIPTION:

Pioneer Days offers a wide variety of events that can be held in a park setting or, even more appropriately, in a community that wants to promote its restoration efforts. Begin Pioneer Days with the arrival of the trail riders and wagon train, who are completing a four hour ride from the "outskirts" of town. (Pre-registration of $15.00 is required and includes tickets for drinks and barbecue.)

RELATED ACTIVITIES:

Depending on the number of days for the event, plan some of the following events: parade with horse drawn wagons and sheriff's posses, fiddlers contest, storytellers, Miss Pioneer Days Contest, bands, (country, western, bluegrass, dixieland), arts and crafts (include sale of gold and silver jewelry, embossed leather), cookoffs (chili, fajitas, barbeque), living history encampment, knife and tomahawk demonstra-

tions, Stockyard Stampede or Depot Day Dash (road race), and Little Buckaroo Corral where cowboys and cowgirls (12 and under) can learn how to rope or make a lasso and then practice. Teach Western crafts like bolo ties and concho head key rings. Each child who visits the corral receives an official certificate making her (or him) "a true saddle pal and amigo of the Old West." Include activities such as muzzle-wading, rifle and frontier hunting skills, basket weaving, candle making, loom weaving, paper making, butter churning, quilting, folkcrafts. Encourage visitor participation and let them try their hand at spinning, weaving, grinding corn or accompany a foot-stompin' rendition of "Rocky Top" on jug band instruments.

CREATIVE PROMOTIONS:

Sell a $3.00 commemorative admission pin, in advance, that will serve as a three-day admission pass.

Southern Travel Magazine, July/August 1988, Fort Worth, Texas

PIG DAY

Includes a hog-calling contest, Little Miss Piglet Contest (longest pigtails) pork cook-off, crafts and food booths.

SWEETCORN AND WATERMELON FESTIVAL

Unusual components include "shuck off" (husking sweetcorn) contest, cooking the corn with an old fashioned steam engine and then serving the corn with watermelon.

COAL FESTIVAL

Mining equipment displays, coal crafts.

ITALIAN FEST

Wine tasting, pizza eating contest, bocci ball, grape stomping and a costume parade are all a part of an Italian affair.

GET COMFORTABLE WITH THE ARTS DAY

DESCRIPTION:

Dispel the notion in your community that the arts are elitist and demonstrate they are for everyone, in some form or another. Businesses encourage their employees to come to work dressed comfortably and casually and give everyone who participates a large button that says "I'm Comfortable With The Arts." The $2.00 button serves as admission to an outdoor concert held downtown that evening, directly after work. Free refreshments are served. This event is especially welcomed in the summertime when everyone enjoys "being cool."

RELATED ACTIVITIES:

Encourage participating businesses to sponsor lunch-hour performances by local artists/musicians or by their own employees, exhibits on their premises or an employee arts and crafts show. How about the children of employee's art show or a creative cooking show down? Sponsor a costume contest for the most comfortably dressed participant(s).

MATERIALS:

Buttons, coupon books for beverages at evening concert.

RESOURCES:

Get the cooperation of any/all of the following: Arts Council, Small Business Committee (Chamber of Commerce), Downtown Association. Contact businesses, including hospitals, newspaper offices, sporting goods, banks, etc.

CREATIVE PROMOTIONS:

Send press kit to the media and include a black and white photo of several people dressed comfortably (beach clothes, cut off sleeves and pants of a "good" suit) and carrying articles such as paint brushes and palette and musical instruments. Send businesses an invitational brochure and registration form. Be sure to ask them how many buttons they want and if they need assistance in contacting a performer or group to entertain at their place of business.

Metropolitan Arts Council, P.O. Box 6401, Greenville, SC 29602

Get Comfortable With The Arts Day!

MEMPHIS IN MAY EXTENSION

Most community center participants do not have the opportunity to go to the downtown arts celebration in Memphis (Memphis in May), so, the center plans a one day event during the festival that is held at the center and in the surrounding neighborhood community. Children parade within the community wearing their basketball uniforms and painters caps. They return to the center to be part of a talent show, a basketball game or skating activity. They feel a part of the larger celebration that is going on downtown.

WE THE PEOPLE CRAFT FAIR

Craft fair featuring country, colonial and contemporary handcrafted items.

SCOTTISH FESTIVAL

DESCRIPTION:

Transform a park or other suitable area into a mini-Scotland, providing an opportunity for Scottish descendants to trace their roots and relive their Scottish heritage. Invite clans to set up an area where those of Scotland descent can come to find out more about their heritage. Festival activities include Scottish singers, dancers, bagpipe bands, games, poetry reading, kilt-making, arts and crafts, traditional music, sheep shearing, blacksmithing, Scottish foods, haggis hurling, films of Scotland, and hayrides.

RELATED ACTIVITIES:

Larger Scottish festivals that have access to more space can hold the traditional Scottish competitive games, Scottish dance competition and the clan procession. Main Stage concerts bring together all of the bagpipe bands, singers, and dancers for a grand performance.

RESOURCES:

Local Scottish society , bagpipe bands, folk dance groups.

MATERIALS:

Stage, Scottish films/videos, projector, VCR, screen or large television.

CREATIVE PROMOTIONS:

Use the voice of a Scot for radio public service announcements.

Nancy Callahan, Greenville Co. Recreation Commission, 500 Roper Mountain Road, Greenville, SC 29615

CELEBRATE MATURITY

An arts and crafts sale and exhibition of seasoned professionals (50 years or older).

FIBER JUBILEE

Presentations and demonstrations showing the processes of raw fiber to finished products, with demonstrations of natural dyeing, carding, spinning and weaving, with various natural fibers such as mohair, wool, angora, linen, cotton and silk.

PIONEER FESTIVAL

Men and women in period costumes demonstrate or exhibit the following: spinning, weaving, butter churning, lace making, wood carving, chair caneing, blacksmithing, basketweaving, china painting, sheepshearing, coppering, soapmaking, broom making, woodworking, molasses making, apple butter making, flax preparati on and dying and preparing food for storage. Offers hands-on activities such as dipping candles, making a rope and participation in pioneer games. Entertainment could include a string band and square dancing. Have homemade bread and apple cider available.

SUPERMAN CELBRATION

Includes Miss Supergirl Beauty Pageant, Superman softball orbaseball tournament, superdog contest, Little Miss Supergirl Pageant, tug-of-war competition between majorindustries/businesses in area, model railroad exhibition and a mock bank robbery.

ASPARAGUS FESTIVAL

Celebration of the year's first crop; fresh picked asparagus for sale.

CITRUS FESTIVAL

Includes a product costume contest, parade of oranges, fiddlers contest.

INVITATIONAL CLAM CHOWDER FESTIVAL

Who makes the greatest clam chowder? Include separate categories for restaurants and individuals and have competition in three divisions: Boston Clam Chowder, Manhattan Clam Chowder and New Jersey Clam Chowder.

COTTON PICKIN' COUNTRY FAIR

Antiques, arts and crafts fair held in old cotton ginning complex with authenic 1890 Victorian home and plenty of country cooking.

ZOOBILEE

Welcome back "vacationing" winter animals with a spring celebration at your zoo.

WET
AND WILD....

AQUATICS

BEST TAN CONTEST

DESCRIPTION:

Pass down the suntan lotion and get your body bronzed for this "tan-talizing" event! Special "summertime" prizes will be awarded, with the grand prize winner receiving a free 4 month pass to the local tanning salon.

RELATED ACTIVITIES:

Miss Pink Tomato Contest (see page 19).

MATERIALS:

Score sheets, clipboards (for the judges), prizes, PA system, stage, number/name badges for each contestant.

POSSIBLE RESOURCES:

Local tanning salons, suntan lotion companies and distributors, companies that sell sunglasses, visors, and beach towels; local chefs of chicken and seafood take-out restaurants (...they're experts on "basting"). Local morticians to judge the "palest" tans; get local barbers to judge the "golden dome" category and local shoe salesmen to judge the whitest feet.

CREATIVE PROMOTIONS:

Make PA announcements, periodically, at the local swimming pools, beaches and health clubs.

JUDGING CATEGORIES:

Darkest tan, most distinct tan line, most even tan, worst sunburn, best t-shirt tan, best left arm tan (for truck drivers who never get to the beach), palest ring finger, best "golden dome" (for bald headed people), best tanned back of the neck, most evenly tanned calves and underfeet, best designs (for people who paste cut outs on their body and lay in the sun), best freckled tan, best dot-to-dot design (connect the freckles), miscellaneous category (for anyone who has anything else to show the judges... within the boundaries).

KEG RODEO

Throw an empty beer keg in a pool or lake. Contender climbs on keg and rides it for a pre-determined time. Person staying on the longest wins. It's different; but it can be done.

AQUA FITNESS

This is an excellent opportunity for men and women to stretch, tone the muscles and improve the body's aerobic system. Water creates resistance, which makes you work hard, yet supports the body, preventing those aches and pains incurred from exercising on dry land.

Aurora Parks & Recreation, Aurora, CD; Course Trends

LIFEGUARD COMPETITION

DESCRIPTION:

Lifeguards! "Man your buoys!" This competition begins with the sound of a gun and includes relay races, diving, deck competition, a jogging relay, and a water volleyball game. The relay race will require 4 guards from each city/team to swim one length of the pool. The first length is done using a lifesaving stroke; second, in an innertube or raft; third, using the corkscrew stroke; and the fourth, using the cross chest carry (two team members are involved). The diving event requires the guards to jump feet first from a high dive into a hula hoop floating in the water. One point is given for each team member passing through the center of the hoop. The deck event resembles a water version of horseshoes. The guards must toss a ring buoy over a stake which floats in the water. The jogging relay requires each guard to jog one length of the pool (shallow end - width). The first member in each team must jog wearing a sweatshirt; the second, wearing sweatpants; the third, wearing tennis shoes; and the fourth, wearing the sweatshirt, sweatpants and the tennis shoes. The round robin volleyball tournament requires three lifeguards from each team competing.

MATERIALS:

PA system, lane lines, ring buoys, floating stakes, sweatshirts, sweatpants, tennis shoes, hula hoops, water volleyball set, innertubes/rafts, scoreboard.

POSSIBLE RESOURCES:

American Red Cross, local high school and college aquatic directors/swim team coaches, local swimming pools and beaches.

Lifesaving Resources, 8403 Cedar Falls Court, Springfield, VA 22153

CREATIVE PROMOTIONS:

Flyers in the shape of ring buoys, or graphic of ring buoy on flyer.

JUDGING CATEGORIES:

See above. Scoring system for each event: 1st Place = 10 points
2nd Place = 7 points
3rd Place = 5 points
4th Place = 3 points

POOLSIDE GANG

Once a month bring your pool participants together for swimming and eating. Everyone brings a covered dish to eat after the swim. Decide on a theme -- all salads, all brunch items, all Italian, etc. While everyone eats, have models around the tables modeling latest swim and outdoor fashions. Schedule a quick-fix hairstyle demonstration.

LIFEGUARD COMPETITION

DESCRIPTION:

Work in conjuction with the local Red Cross to implement this aquatic event, which will promote and perfect safety in your area. Invite area lifeguards to a water site or pool to compete in water safety and First Aid skills. Participants are judged in three areas -- water safety skills, (approach, quick reverse, escapes and releases), First Aid skills (treatment of neck and back, and head injuries, rescue breathing, use of backboard and rescue tube), and strokes (modified crawl, side and breast).

RELATED ACTIVITIES:

Present awards at a cookout following the event.

MATERIALS:

Normal first aid supplies, rescue tube, trophies or prizes, t-shirts for all participants.

POSSIBLE RESOURCES:

Red Cross, area pools, hotels and motels, community clubs, recreation departments, lakes and beaches. Local sporting goods store as sponsor.

DRINK SPLASH

The objective is for participants to retrieve drinks in cans from the bottom of the pool. Place participants around the pool in various areas where they can enter the pool quickly. Throw a variety of brands of cold drinks in the pool (singles or six packs, depending on number of participants). Blow a whistle and let participants jump/dive in and collect what they can or want. Variations include: collecting one of each kind; 2 person teams tied together at the wrists; stacking cans.

POOLSIDE STUFF IT

Several gross of ping pong balls are in the pool. The females fill their suits with as many balls as possible. The event is timed and the person with the most balls in their suit wins.

SURF, SUN & SAND

DESCRIPTION:

Here's a chance to combine several water special events into one entire day of Fun! The day begins with windsurfing competition and demos, followed by an afternoon Best Tan Contest (see page 16) and ends with the judging of a sand castle building contest.

RELATED ACTIVITIES:

Beach volleyball tourney, Miss Pink Tomato Contest (see page 19), windsurfing lessons, body surfing, leg contest.

MATERIALS:

Volleyball net and balls, rakes, boundary markers.

POSSIBLE RESOURCES:

Local surf shop, beach patrol and lifeguards, local architect group to act as judges for sand castle building contest.

MISS PINK TOMATO CONTEST

This is a best tan contest for little girls 3-5 years old. Judging categories could include those listed in "Best Tan Contest" (see page 16), plus cutest bikini, cutest one-piece bathing suit, cutest beach outfit, cutest smile. Prizes could include inflatable water toys, beach buckets, beach balls, and a basket of cherry tomatos (instead of a bouquet of flowers) for the overall winner...Miss Pink Tomato.

WHITE WATER RAFTING TRIP

Plan a trip for your thrill seekers with a high adventure white water rafting trip. Contact an area river outfitter who will provide a professional guide. Lunch is also provided.

SPLISH SPLASH WATER BASH

Plan a day centered around water activities. This is a great event for centers without pools or for any hot summer day. Include a water balloon toss where a balloon is tossed between two people until it eventually breaks on the "lucky" person. Make a "slip and slide" from heavy duty polyurethane plastic, liquid detergent and water. Have ice sitting contests, ice on the tummy endurance competitions and just plain ole' squirt the kids with a hose. Ask a fire department to come on the scene to squirt water from a fire hose. End the festivities with a cookout.

TOPLESS BATHING SUIT COMPETITION

Get the cooperation of the most progressive radio station in your market to sponsor the topless bathing suit competition. What you keep a secret is the fact that contestants are men.

WINTER POOL PARTY

Warmer climates or indoor heated pools can "break the ice" and boredom of winter with a pool party featuring swimming, water games, polar cups (frozen drinks), ice cream churning and a visit from the polar bear.

FISHING DERBY

If you are looking for an exciting finale to your pool season, here is your chance! Let your pool water stand without chemicals for about one week. Order 300 pounds of catfish, and sell tickets to the public. Fishermen of all ages and abilities will show. Have some fishing equipment for rent.

ANYTHING THAT FLOATS RACE

Participants - individual and/or team -- race from one side of a lake or river to the other side. Entries cannot be real boats or motor driven. Entries can be 55 gallon drums, innertubes, port-o-lets, bathtubs, wooden or styrofoam struc tures. In addition to awarding prizes for 1st, 2nd, and 3rd to finishers, present awards to most original, smallest, largest, slowest, most ridiculous.

WACKY WATER OLYMPICS

Teams compete for the most points in the following water activities: carry an egg on a spoon from one side of the pool to the other; dive for coins within a time period; Wet Scavenger Hunt (see below); kick board race; walking on hands under water; relay race; blow up balloon(s) under water; blow ping pong ball across pool.

BELLY COLORING CONTEST

As part of a swimming or pool event, schedule a time for belly coloring, using watercolors, finger paints or soap paints. Judge for most colorful and most creative design.

WET SCAVENGER HUNT

This event accomodates all age levels depending on "where" the objects are placed. Some objects -- pennies and rings; for instance, are thrown to the bottom for older swimmers. Younger swimmers can vie for floating objects and items placed around the edge of the pool. Each contestant accumulates his items on his towel for the final total. Wet Scavenger Hunt can be played with individual contestants, teams or a parent-child team, in the case of younger participants.

Linda Pearson, Spartanburg YMCA, Spartanburg, SC

ROMPER STOMPERS....

PRE-SCHOOL

STUFFED ANIMAL CONTEST

DESCRIPTION:

It's time to clear off your bed and bring your favorite stuffed animal out for a day of fun...just for them! Participants will have the opportunity to have their stuffed animals judged in several different categories.

RELATED ACTIVITIES:

Have a "tea party" after the judging for all participants and their animals.

MATERIALS:

Measuring tape, PA system, stage area, contestant name badges, judging sheets, prizes.

POSSIBLE RESOURCES:

Local toy stores, children's stores.

JUDGING CATEGORIES:

Biggest eyes, floppiest ears, best musical animal, smallest, largest, best Teddy Bear, longest tongue, most "worn out," oldest.

JOLLY "GREEN" GIANT DAY

DESCRIPTION:

Everything that is done on this day is done in a giant manner. Contestants participate in a giant ring toss (using hula-hoops), giant golf (using oversized plastic golf clubs from the toy store), and giant volleyball (using a large beachball instead of a volleyball.) Contestants should come dressed in over-sized, green clothing and shoes.

MATERIALS:

Hula-hoops, plastic golf clubs, golf course tees and greens (make your own in a local park), beachball, volleyball court, stakes for hula-hoop ring toss, PA system, score cards for each participant, plastic softball-sized whiffle balls for giant golf.

POSSIBLE RESOURCES:

Local golf courses, toy stores, Green Giant vegetable company.

JUDGING CATEGORIES:

Lowest golf score, highest ring toss score, best two out of three in volleyball.

HOLIDAY ANKLEBITERS

Parents can Christmas shop while their children enjoy quality activities and Christmas crafts.

LITTLE THIS 'N' THAT

This is a creative recreation program for 3 1/2 - 5 years olds. Activities include circle time, little schools, video, songs and games, cooking crafts, lunch time, and playground.

CHOO CHOO CONSTRUCTION

DESCRIPTION:

Pre-schoolers create "boxcars" from cardboard boxes. Wheels are small paper plates; boxes are colored with bright tempera's; name plates are attached.

RELATED ACTIVITIES:

Sing songs having to do with railroads; read stories about trains, such as "The Little Engine Who Could." Use electrical tape to form train tracks.

MATERIALS:

Small paper plates, multi-colored temperas, cardboard boxes, construction paper, glue, markers, electrical tape.

POSSIBLE RESOURCES:

Pre-schools and parents.

Darlene Buchanan, City of Anniston, AL

WEE-BOWL DAY

When it's "bowl game time" for adults every New Year season, make it a special bowl day for pre-school age children. Begin the day by displaying and making a paper bowl hat. Activities are centered around anything about bowls: how they're made; what goes in them; what they can be used for and stories about bowls. Use bowls for math and creative writing or speaking exercises; include how many beans are in the bowl contest; how many words can be spelled from B, O, W, and L; who can list the most uses of a bowl in five minutes; tell the funniest thing you can think of to put in a bowl - then draw it.

WEE WATCHERS

Have pre-schoolers make their own binoculars to be used on bird watching outings. Familiarize them with common birds through coloring exercises and short lessons. Compile small picture bird books and have the little bird watchers check off the birds as they see them. Binoculars are made with two tissue rolls glued together. Let them sit overnight, then paint and punch a small hole on each side and string on a neck strap with yarn.

SOOOO BIG

As part of your pre-school program, offer "soooo big" activities to acquaint the children with household responsibilities such as, "cooking" and cleaning up afterwards. Teach them the art of making a peanut butter and jelly sandwich and getting their own glass of milk. The second part of the lesson is cleaning up the mess. For woodworking, bring in scraps of wood and nails, hammers, screws and screwdrivers, and let the little carpenters "build" away. They will come up with some great structures. Begin each day with an exercise routine to include warmups, stretching, arms and legs, waist, tummy, walking, and cool down. For gardening and/or houseplants, plant a preschool garden and everyone can reap the harvest. Plant carrots, radishes, cucumbers, and then make a salad. Let each student be responsible for an indoor plant; have watering day and instruct them on plant maintenance. For car washing, let them practice on your car and the staff's cars. For sweeping, invest in small brooms and have the tots sweep certain areas on a consistent basis. For fire safety, invite a city fireman in to speak on fire safety and have each child draw him a thank you note.

THE GLAD SCIENTISTS

Young scientists (4-5 year olds) explore the wonders of magnetism, light, air, water, energy and more through observation and experimentation.

GULLIVER'S TRAVELS

Pre-schoolers, ages 3-4, have fun learning important skills related to their world. Songs, games, stories and projects are centered around different weekly themes to include animals, weather, and transportation.

JELLY BEAN FIELD DAY

Children go to stations of their choice and complete tasks of various difficulty. When a task is accomplished they receive a jelly bean. Events can range from coloring a picture to doing a cartwheel.

TINY TOT OLYMPICS

Three, four, and five year olds participate in events such as the big wheel race, the obstacle course, tee-ball hit, bean bag throw. Everyone who participates gets a goodie bag with small toy prizes and candy. Every one is a winner.

MAGIC TRICKS "A LA PEANUT BUTTER SANDWICHES"

Children , ages 5 - 7 are accompanied by one or two enthusiastic parents. The children learn 5 magic tricks and then perform in a real magic show. Participants bring articles required by instructor, such as a deck of cards, silky square scarf, coins, etc.

Williamsville Central Schools, East Amherst, NC Course Trends.

TEDDY BEAR PICNIC AT THE ZOO

Bring your teddy bears to the zoo for a parade and picnic. Show your teddy bear off at the teddy bear showcase and bring him to the "Quickwell Clinic" for a check-up and/or repair.

"ONCE UPON A TIME"

Schedule weekly gatherings in the park, under a large tree, where children and parents come to hear storytellers. Some storytellers might bring props and costumes and ask the children to act out the story.

LOLLIPOP CONCERTS

Introduce young children to the classics and musical instruments in this monthly series at the library.

OREO OLYMPICS

This is a cookie competition for 3 - 8 year olds. Divide contestants into age groups and run competitions in oreo stacking, oreo rolling, relays and eating. Ribbons are awarded.

STICKY FINGERS

Select projects where kids can get their hands "dirty"! Messy crafts, paints, dough and paper mache can be used. Stress participation and creativity. Bring Dad's old shirt or a smock.

DEFINITELY TWO

This is carefully designed creative play centering on developing social skills and having fun in an all 2-year old group.

DOLL SHOW AND TEA PARTY

Youngsters 11 years old and younger are invited to bring their "babies" out for a Doll Show. During the judging all youngsters will enjoy attending a dress-up tea party. Participants will also have fun competing in a costume parade so pull out your fanciest apparel and jewelry. Time will also be allotted for cupcake decorating, jewelry making, a fashion show, and games. Categories for doll judging include: Best: stuffed, character, teenager doll, rag doll, handmade doll, old fashioned doll, clown doll, foreign doll, most unusual doll, most interesting pair of dolls, and a prize for the doll who has "come the furthest."

MINI-TRACK MEET

Kids love to run and jump, so why not a track and field meet just for them. Schedule different length runs, short hurdles and a throwing contest. This event could be incorporated with a diaper derby and/or Big Wheel Rally.

TEAM ART

Select several art projects that parent(s) and child can enjoy creating together and schedule a six week (one day a week) session for the team work. Suggested crafts: clay, mosaic trivots, tie dye, batik. This can be offered as part of a pre-school program or programmed independently.

Here are some creative names for other pre-school activities:

Small Fry Olympics	Mommy and Me	Tiny Tot Tumbling	Kindercooks
Paint, Paste, and Paper	Art Experiences	Young Children's Games	Time for Twos
First Aid for Little People	Pre-school Olympics	Parent/Tot Rollerskating	Gym-Nee-Crickets
Little People's Projects	Tot Fiesta	Itty Bitty Basketball	Tiny Tappers
Short Chef Creations	Koffee and Krayons	Tiny Tots Ice	Little Sprouts
Pipsqueak PE	Social Sandbox	Fairy Tales & Fables	Kindergym and
Exploration Station	Safety Town	Midget Masterpieces	Kiddie Lit
Button-sized Ballerinas	Let's Pretend	Cutting, Gluing, and Painting	Head over Heels
Infant Massage	Creative Playtime	Whoop-Dee-Doo	Wee Chef
Playin' Around	Silver Spoons	Midget Mania	Crafty Critters
Nimble Fingers	Tiny Tot Tuneland	Alphabet Soup	Safe and Sound
Mighty Marching Mini-Band	Toddler's Night Out	Dyna-Mite Hockey	Two Timers
Creation Stations	Tots and Trikes	Sports Sampler	Craft Hour
Kids in the Kitchen	Bubbles, Rainbows, and Worms		
Mighty Might Curtain Climber's Club			

KIDS
KORNER....

YOUTH

INVENTION CONVENTION*

DESCRIPTION:

An Invention Convention is designed to develop critical and creative thinking skills among students by encouraging them to create an invention. This can be a major community-wide event, held at small recreation centers, or as part of a summer program. A couple of creative, workable inventions include the Grocery Shuttle and Surprizer Organizer. The Grocery Shuttle is a portable, collapsible, triangular frame that can be set up inside the car. It has hooks that plastic grocery bags are placed on, thus preventing the contents from scattering around the car. A Surprizer Organizer is a lifesize plywood cutout of a teenager and is designed so its owner can "clothe" it with the planned wardrobe for the next day. * In conjuction with a nationwide event-- Invent America.

RELATED ACTIVITIES:

Charge admission to the public to view inventions. Arrange for an area inventor to speak to the young inventors.

MATERIALS:

Students supply their own or present a material list to you.

JUDGING CATEGORIES:

Most resourceful, most useful, most practical, most convenient, most frivilious, most elaborate.

MINI-MARATHON

This is a marathon of small events. Two teams of any age compete in events (watermelon eating, frisbee toss, basketball throw, raisin count, etc.). There are usually 20 to 25 events. Each child is stationed at an event. When one child finishes an event, he/she runs to the next station and begins that event; and it continues until all events are completed.

SUPER SPLITS

What better way to beat the heat than a giant banana split? Set up four to five banquet tables in a row. Place four to five 10 foot plastic rain gutters in line so there is one long gutter on each side of the table. Line gutters with foil and fill with ice cream. Children select their own toppings from the variety of condiments brought in by those who responded to a letter sent home to the parents asking for contributuons (whipped cream, nuts, cherries, syrups). Gutters are easy to wash out and may be saved for years. If your group is large, seat the children in shifts. Meanwhile, offer face painting or another activity to those who are waiting for their treat. An added activity could be to make homemade ice-cream earlier in the day.

Lakeland Recreation Department, Lakeland, Florida

KIDS KAMPS

Offer courses at your recreation center that provide fun while learning. Use your staff and contracted instructors as the teachers. The following courses could be offered independently or as a summer program where the young students select several activities. Suggested programs: Tennis Anyone?, Computers, Krazy Krafts for Kids, Gymastics, First Dance: Ballet, Tiny Tumblers, Horseback Riding, Golf, Swimming, Fun with Science, Drawing/Right Side of Brain, Drawing Cartoons, Discover the Abstract, Drawing Beyond the Pencil, Making Art on the Computer, Skateboarding, Diving, Tennis.

Furman University, Greenville, SC 29613

BICYCLE WEEK

DESCRIPTION:

Cycling is quickly becoming more popular among all age groups and all levels of achievement.   Activities to be considered during Bicycle Week would be: early evening fun rides, weekend touring, bike parade, bike parade, three-wheel rides, tricycle race, 1 and 2 miles races for children and adults, historic bike tour, criterion races (professional touring races) and cross country road races, from 30 to 100 miles.

RELATED ACTIVITIES:

Conduct a poster contest prior to event, using the best posters to promote the event. Photo contest after event to be used in next year's publicity.

MATERIALS:

Flyers listing schedule of week's events, first aid kits.

POSSIBLE RESORCES:

Bicycle clubs and stores, bicycle race association, YMCA, YWCA, police, fire departments, EMS, civic organizations.

CREATIVE PROMOTIONS:

Encourage local newspaper to run a feature on bicycle awareness called "Bicycles Are Vehicles," stressing cyclist's rights and announcing the week long events.

JUDGING CATEGORIES:

Poster contest, photo contest (most original, best drawing, best theme interpretation of "Bicycles Are Vehicles.")

Pat Cadle, Southern Pines Recreation and Parks Departments, Box 870, Southern Pines, NC 28387

NATURE TREK

Open your park for a Nature Trek Series to be held on a Saturday once a month during February, March, April, and May. Each month the focus will be on a different topic in nature. Examples of topics could include how birds of prey, snakes, spiders, and butterflies live in their natural environment. Art activities and nature games work well to help children understand and enjoy the sessions. Invite yor local State Park Naturalist in as speaker.

Judi Dorsey, Sesquicentennial State Park, 9564 Two Notch Road, Columbia, SC 29223

VEGETABLE CREATONS

Bring Mr. Potato Head to life with a exercise in vegetable and fruit creations. Your local grocer can contribute old produce for the event. Use larger produce (potatoes, eggplant, squash) for the base, and smaller produce and leafy greens for features and toothpicks for security to complete a face, animal or inanimate object (no carving allowed). Creations could be judged on creativity, attention to detail and unusual names.

EVERYDAY IS A HOLIDAY

DESCRIPTION:

The only thing wrong with holidays is that they only come once a year! You can make them happen twice. Choose the five favorites and plan all day activities for each. Schedule art projects, games, contests, food and traditional activities for Christmas, Halloween, Easter, Valentines, Thanksgiving, 4th of July or St. Patrick's Day.

RELATED ACTIVITIES:

Christmas: everyone brings an unbroken toy from home to be wrapped in wrapping paper that was made in art class; Halloween: elaborate mask making; Easter: have a parade; Valentines: make Valentines or a heart mobile, or how about candy making? Thankgiving: plant a garden; 4th of July: join in on the communitiy's festivities and for St. Patricks' Day, make it a completely green day.

MATERIALS:

Art supplies, Santa suit, candy, game books, records and stereo/ tapes, foods and other supplies, relative to chosen holidays.

POSSIBLE RESOURCES:

Arts and crafts books, game books, library.

CREATIVE PROMOTIONS:

Display a large sign with enjoyable graphics to remind the participants of what each day will celebrate. Also indicate whether or not they are to bring anything from home, i.e., Christmas gift, Easter basket.

JUDGING CATEGORIES:

Parade entries, Halloween costumes, Valentine design, patriotic poster contest, egg hunt.

JUMPING JACK JAM

Each person stands up in front to tell a story. Everytime he/she says a word beginning with B (or what ever letter is chosen), the listeners have to do 3 or 5 jumping jacks.

BAZOOKA JOE BONANZA

This event uses Bazooka bubblegum in activities such as a gum blowing contest, Bazooka Pitch, and Bazooka Relay. Include famous "knock-knock" jokes and a "dress like Joe" contest. Decorate using Red, White and Blue. Bazooka Pitch - Set up a bucket a distance away from the participants. Each person gets 10 pieces of gum. The person who gets the most pieces in the bucket is the winner. Bazooka Relay - The first player on each team is given two toothpicks. A piece of wrapped Bazooka is on the floor in front of him/ her. He/She must pick up the piece of gum between the toothpicks and race to the end of course and come back with it and hand it over to the next teammate in line. If the piece is dropped it must be picked up with the toothpicks. (No fair sticking the picks into the gum or under the wrapper to hold it.) Bazooka Stacking Contest - Everyone takes a turn in stacking pieces of bubble gum, one on top of the other. The one who makes the biggest pile before it topples is the winner.

Topps Chewing Gum, Inc., P.O. Box 300, Westbury, NY 11590

FANTASY FUN FESTIVAL

DESCRIPTION:

It's a world of make believe for children, kindergarden through 7th grade who participate in "Fantasy Island." Fantasies could include: Space Exploration (be an astronaut, explore the stars and planets and study spaceships); Tom Sawyer (explore nature and study trees, streams, animals, rocks, plants); Hollywood (become an actor, director, writer, cameraman, or producer); Olympics (be a participant in the Olympics); Computers (enter the world of computers); Jungle Safari (travel through a jungle and learn about tribal dance and backpacking); Circus (be a circus acrobat by learning gymnastic skills); 20,000 Leagues Under the Sea (become Captain Nemo and explore the ocean depths); Culinary delights (bake pizza, decorate a cake); Artist (create your own fantasy with arts and crafts); Aerobic dance (learn one of today's most popular dances). Certain fantasies are limited to appropriate age groups and a child chooses three of the fantasies and one alternate.

RELATED ACTIVITIES:

Schedule field trips and guest speakers that relate to respective fantasies.

MATERIALS:

Art materials, reference books, costumes, game and sports equipment, camping equipment, gym mats, submarine, kitchen, record player, records, boom box, cassettes, film, video, screen.

POSSIBLE RESORCES:

Planetarium and guide, historic museum director, environmentalist, community theatre director or high school drama teacher, computer center, computer programmer, Sierra club, clown, circus performers, pizza chef, baker, candlestick maker, aerobic teacher.

CREATIVE PROMOTIONS:

Use Fantasy Island motif in written and vocal public service announcements.

Lynda Baer and Alma Withers, Fredericksburg Parks and Recreation Department, 1103 Kenmore Ave., Fredericksburg, VA.

AFTERNOON ACADEMY

By collaborating with the public schools, your department can provide an enriching after school program at local schools. Ages K through 14 can attend classes taught by public school teachers or other contracted professionals. Popular activities include sports, ceramics, languages, model airplane workshop, computers, building bird house feeders, ballroom dance. In the television workshop children grades K - 6 write and direct a program on the local television station. Little Feet is the after school aerobics, and along with ballet and art programs is a popular class. The average cost is $5.00 per hour.

Montgomery County Recreation Department, Tiburon, CA

SATURDAY SKATE AROUND

Convert your recreation center into a skating rink by using the gym, a large room or opening up several rooms into one. Set up cones to make a rink. Simulate a skating rink by providing music, popcorn and a variety of skating rink games.

Susan Miller, Virginia Beach Recreation Center - Bow Creek 3427 Club House Road, Virginia Beach, VA 23462

MEDIEVAL FAIR

DESCRIPTION:

Make the Middle Ages come alive at a medieval fair for the youth in your community. The sixth graders at an elementary school in Spartanburg, SC produced a medieval fair at their school, and the event can be duplicated on a recreation park level, as long as enough children and adults are commited. The day-long event begins with a Parade of Colors and Coronation of a King and Queen. The young hosts and hostesses create and wear costumes of the Middle Ages (long dresses, tunics, wreaths, pointed hats, armor). They also present Medieval folk dancing, a Maypole dance, jousting and a play (all of which have been taught by a contracted professional or teachers). Adults set up the Medieval village, complete with bread baking, stain glass window making, calligraphy, chess tournaments, puppetry, archery demonstrations, and mock sword fights. Everyone has the opportunity to trade their unwanted possessions for treasures at a trade farm.

RELATED ACTIVITIES:

Include a feast, complete with roasted pork, vegetables, fruit, bread, pastries, and, in medieval tradition, no forks are used. Dinner entertainment can include music, a jester and proclaimations (awards) from distant queens. Depending on the resources and how elaborate you choose to make this affair you could coordinate the event to the extent of a structured learning experience four to five weeks prior. Students could study the Medieval period through resource books, social studies textbooks and films. Provide speakers (from the Society of Creative Anachronism to demonstrate articles peculiar to the Middle Ages). Have students assist in constructing decorations and props for the affair.

Sarah Wheeler/Nancy Finkell, E.P. Todd Elementary School, Spartanburg, SC.

BIKE RODEO

DESCRIPTION:

Contact your local Sheriff's Office or Police Department to assist with this safety program. Before the rodeo begins, participants are each given a cowboy hat bearing the sponsor's name. Events include a video presentation on bicycle safety, bicycle inspections, competition on an obstacle course, and instruction on how to change a flat tire. After the rodeo, the participants go on a mile group ride to use their new skills. They will then receive a bicycle registration tag from the the Sheriff's department.

RELATED ACTIVITIES:

Rodeo clown, BMX demonstration, new bicycle give-a-way, bicycle auction (confiscated bicycles from police department), big wheel race for younger sibblings.

MATERIALS:

VCR, television, cones, barricades, certificates, registration table, registration forms, bicycle registration tags.

POSSIBLE RESOURCES:

Sheriff or Police Department, bike shops, Boy and Girl Scout troops, schools.

CREATIVE PROMOTIONS:

Plan event for American Bike Month (May) and begin advertising by holding a poster contest in the area schools. Posters would advertise the Bike Rodeo event.

WACKY OLYMPICS

For a real change of pace, plan a Wacky Olympics! Include events such as the: rubber chicken throw, shoe kick, marshmallow shot put, straw javelin, paper plate discus; Swimming events, greased water melon haul, ping pong ball blowing, rescue - a - brick, bathtub sit-in (how many people can fit into one bathtub); play softball with a ping pong ball, and include armless events (tie arms behind backs). Other events could include:

BIG BALL VOLLEY -
Use beach-size ball and follow regular volleyball rules or take as many hits as needed.
BLINDFOLD PUTTING CONTEST-
Putt goft ball blindfolded.

CLOTHES HANGER RELAY -
Have three two-man teams. The object of the race is to fill one finger on each hand with ten hangers. At the count of 3, run and meet your teammate. You are to exchange hangers from your fingers to his without touching the hangers. (Let the hangers slide from your fingers to your teammates fingers). The team that finishes the race with the most hangers still on their fingers wins. Fingers must be straight at all times.
ZIP STRIP (relay style) -
First person runs about 20 yards, gets into a sleeping bag, takes off his/her clothes and puts on the clothes in the bag, then runs back to tag the next person in line. Each person on the team will follow until each person has changed clothes. First team to finish wins.

"P" PARTY

Take any letter of the alphabet and center all activities around that letter. For "P," have a Pancake Relay; dress up as a "P" something (a pickle, in pajamas); eat "P" food (peas, peanut butter); win "P" prizes; and, of course, take p-ictures of the events and activities.

FASHION DAY

Participants (boys and girls) bring their "very best outfit," make-up and hot rollers and then spend one hour dressing up and primping. Everyone then attends a fashion show and tea party. The other kids are the judges and prizes are awarded.

CHEMISTRY KIDS

Using common house-hold ingredients, 6 - 8 year old students assemble a chemistry kit. Design experiments to grow crystals, test for starches and ph levels, and explore the physical sciences.

BACKWARDS OLYMPICS

Events are performed backwards (running, up slides, down ladders, bat in opposite hand, run bases).

COIFFURE EXCHANGE

The girls choose a partner and plan their hair-dos, for each other. The next day they bring all necessary equipment and style each others hair. Other participants of the program vote for winning entries.

HUCK FINN FISHING TOURNAMENT

DESCRIPTION:
Want to have a "reel" good time? Join us for an afternoon of fishing on the shores of a nearby lake or river. Everyone should come dressed for the occasion (remember what Huck Finn, Tom Sawyer, Becky Thatcher look like?) Children can bring their own cane pole or you can provide them with one.

RELATED ACTIVITIES:
Huck Finn look-a-like contest, raft building, fish fry, catching gold fish in a swimming pool.

MATERIALS:
Cane poles, hooks, line, worms, trophies, ribbons, containers for caught fish.

POSSIBLE RESOURCES:
Area clubs, neighborhoods, schools. Local fish and tackle supply stores and pet stores.

CREATIVE PROMOTIONS:
Display a Huck Finn raft with a cane pole and bucket of gold fish in an appropriate location. Have fishing equipment and straw hats for sale.

JUDGING CATEGORIES:
Biggest fish, most fish caught, longest fish, smallest fish, hardest fish to land, Huck Finn look-a-like, best fishing hat.

Fort Mill Recreation Department, Fort Mill, SC

KALEIDOSCOPE

Offer a children's cultural arts series where participants will sample a variety of activities after school, on Saturdays, or in a day camp situation. Include puppet and/or marionette performance, puppet and/or marionette making workshop followed by script writing, stage making and performance. Include drama, improvisational acting and a play performance; field trip to a symphony and a survey of musical instruments; clown class, mime performance and hands on art activities.

FINGER POETS

Students have a great time learning finger spelling and express short poems, limericks and rhymes in American Sign Language.

CHOCOLATE FACTORY MOVIE AND CANDY CLASS

Rent the movie and afterwards, or on the following day, conduct a candy making class and even a Willie Wonka look-alike contest.

"CATCH A RISING STAR"

Take a talent show one step further and have winners and other promising entrants perform in front of a television camera. Work in conjunction with your local cable company who will film the show and present it on the local cable network.

Virginia Rivers/Angelo Spoto, Tampa Recreation Department, 1420 Tampa Street, Tampa Florida 33602

WINTERFEST/WONDERFUL WINTER WONDERLAND

DESCRIPTION:
Come play with us in the white, powdery snow. The day will include a variety of activities with snow being the main ingredient. Included will be a snowball throw for distance and accuracy, snow painting, tug-of-war through a snow wall, sledding races and contests, ice skating events, obstacle courses, snowball rolling, snowball softball, saucer jumps, snow volleyball, broom-sled races and a snow sculpturing contest. Participants must supply their own favorite sled/saucer.

RELATED ACTIVITIES:
Offer adult cross-country skiing clinics while the above activities are being held for the youngsters.

MATERIALS:
Target for snowball throw, powder paint in dixie cups for snow painting, tug-of-war rope, measuring tape for snowball rolling, flourescent orange softball, bat for snowball softball game, volleyball net, brooms, prizes, PA system.

POSSIBLE RESOURCES:
Local ski shops, ice arenas, schools. Companies that sell sleds and saucers.

CREATIVE PROMOTIONS:
Make posters in the shape of snowmen. Attach a red scarf around the neck and arms made of sticks/twigs.

"RUN AROUND THE CLOCK"

This event can be used with a variety of activities (reading, walking, exercising,, etc.). Each child is given a "clock" or a circle divided into 12 pie pieces. Each time a certain activity is completed (child runs 1/2 mile), the parent or recreation leader signs pie piece. At the end of the activity time period hold a 50's party and present awards for finishers and those who excelled.

BE A CLOWN CAMP

DESCRIPTION:

Here's a chance for children (8 and over) to "run away with the circus" and perform under the "big top." Hire a retired professional clown to conduct a five day workshop, which could include the following: clown history and traditions, development of sense of humor and character, creation of clown personality, unique to an individual (make up design and application, construction of a wig, latex nose, costume.) Also in preparation of the "Biggest Little Show on Earth," participants are taught simple acrobatics, juggling, magic tricks, balloon toys, prat fall and skills.

RELATED ACTIVITIES:

Hold a "Clown for a Day" Workshop for younger participants (5-10), where the professional clown becomes a clown before their very eyes, carefully explaining how to apply makeup, developing a personality and costume. The children then get an opportunity to apply makeup, tell jokes, fall gently and develop their sense of humor.

MATERIALS:

Clown white and other theatrical makeup, request list sent home to include colorful clothing and props, gymnastic mat, weighted tennis balls for juggling, balloons and other items required by clown. Decorations for "Big Top."

POSSIBLE RESOURCES:

Clown College (Venice, Florida), National Clown Association, arts council, community theatre for clown. children's theatre, community theatre, schools and day cares.

CREATIVE PROMOTIONS:

Circus music lead-in on a public service announcement radio spot, hand-made posters (poster contest) made by children, announcing the event.

Marianne Laucis, Recreation Specialist, Irmo Chapin Recreation Commission, 200 Leisure Lane, Columbia, SC 29210

TOTS TEA PARTY/DOLL SHOW & TEA PARTY

DESCRIPTION:

Youngsters 11 years and younger are invited to bring their "babies" out for a Doll Show. During the judging, all youngsters will enjoy attending a dress-up tea party. Participants will also have fun competing in a costume parade, so pull out your fanciest apparel and jewelry. Time will also be alloted for cupcake decorating, jewelry making, a fashion show and games.

POSSIBLE RESOURCES:

Toy stores, children's clothing stores, pre-schools.

JUDGING CATEGORIES:

Best stuffed character, teenage doll, most interesting pair of dolls, best rag doll, best handmade doll, best old-fashioned doll, best clown doll, foreign doll, most unusual doll.

INTERNATIONAL WEEK (GERMANY)

DESCRIPTION:

International Week is great during the summer months. You might choose to "explore" one country or highlight a different country each day. Research can be delegated and also shared between different facilities. Using germany as an example, you could program the following events: begin by showing a scenic tour or educational film of the country; offer art projects each day (garlands, suspenders for lederhaussen, German houses from milk cartons, Christmas ornaments), bratwurst and pretzel lunches, Christmas party, German dances, German music, costume contest, chug-a-lug contest, and a Volksmarch (see page 74) with medals for awards.

RELATED ACTIVITIES:

Share all the fun and knowledge by getting together, in costume with the other facilities. Have a Christmas party with all the countries representing their customs. Present a program to the public demonstrating dances from the different countries. Display art projects at a local mall. Design a Volkswagen Beauty Contest (see page 56).

MATERIALS:

Films, projector, screen, reference books, art supplies, food, records.

POSSIBLE RESOURCES:

Library, local international clubs, German band, school music department.

CREATIVE PROMOTIONS:

Offer a "Around the World Tour" to the public for free.

JUDGING CATEGORIES:

Contest for the following: costume, Volkswagen design, landscape drawing/painting, dance.

MOTOR CAR RALLY

Get a radio station to co-sponsor this event; the dads to build the track; and the kids to race their motorized cars. The track is built with 2' x 4's and cars are judged on times, straight heats, demolitions, and even tractor pulls. Charge an entry fee of $25.00 to cover trophies for the four age groups: 5-6, 7-9, 10-12, and 13 and up.

HOE DOWN

Ages 3 to 10 enjoy dressing in western or country attire and visiting with farm animals that are brought into the recreation center. Plan a simple square dance too.

PRE-TEEN SPEND THE NIGHT

All pre-teens, 6-12 years of age, are invited to stay over for an evening of games, snacks, and breakfast. Activities for the night would include: general play, organized active games, tournaments, movies, midnight swim in the summer, wind down games, such as ghost story telling, charades and refreshment time. Separate rooms for girls and boys sleeping on mats, if available.

Allen Greene, Virginia Beach Recreation Center, 3427 Club House Road, Virginia Beach, VA 23462

CENTER GOLF COURSE

Your center can have its own golf course -- inexpensively, too. Get donations of old clubs, and use plastic balls. Map out a course and have certain "targets" for the players to hit, i.e., a tree, a drinking fountain, a bench leg.

MOM, SON HOE DOWN

Moms and Sons, grab your partners for the Mom and Son Hoe Down. This special event for mothers and sons includes a barbecue, games, contests, door prizes and square dancing.

Largo Recreation and Parks Depts., P.O. Box 296, Largo, Florida 34649-0296.

JUGGLING WORKSHOP AND COMPETITION

If you do not have an experienced juggler on your staff, contract a professional clown, mime or juggler to teach a series of classes to youth teens and even adults. Have a recital of sorts at the end where students and teams of students perform their new skills. Offer prizes for the audiences' favorite jugglers.

JIGSAW PUZZLE CONTEST

Plan a jigsaw puzzle contest as an afternoon activity, all day activity, or run it every afternoon for a week. Each team works the same puzzle if it is a one afternoon event, but if the contest is scheduled for all day or for more than one afternoon, rotate the different puzzles, giving each team a chance at each puzzle. Set a time limit, (2 hours), then total the connecting pieces. The team(s) with the highest total is the winner. Prizes, of course, are jigsaw puzzles or gift certificates at hobby or card shops.

CELEBRITY PHOTO SESSION

Invite local celebrities to your center to meet your children and let the two pose together for a photo. A few days later give the children the opportunity to purchase their favorite photograph. Provide refreshments and a short entertainment program for your guest celebrities.

KRAZY DAZE COMPETITION

DESCRIPTION:

Krazy Daze makes for fun competition between centers or at just one recreation center, if your department is small. Three age groups split up into male and female groups and compete in games and relays in district competition. One center in each district goes to final Krazy Daze Competition. It is important that each center is briefed thoroughly on the standardized rules, in order to assure fairness. Some suggestions for games: Ages 5-8 and 9-12: Ring toss, bubble gum relay (chew gum, blow bubble), 3-legged race, frisbee water carry (on knees, carry a cup of water positioned on a frisbee to the other side and dump the water in a bucket), water balloon toss. Ages 13-16: football free throw, 100 yard inner tube relay (five people in one tube), find your shoes (that are in one big pile) and put them on relay, 50 yard backyard dash.

RELATED ACTIVITIES:

Have buttons for participants that read "I Fit Right Into Krazy Daze." Set up carnival games and concessions.

MATERIALS:

Game and relay supplies, judges sheets, prizes, concessions, P.A. system, stage.

RESOUCES:

Sporting goods store, hobby store or media sponsor. For participation: recreation centers, scout troops, clubs or groups, YMCA, YWCA, day camps.

CREATIVE PROMOTIONS:

Promote as a rival-type competition from the beginning by encouraging teams at the different centers to challenge each other. Have teams give themselves a name.

JUDGING CATEGORIES:

At a closing ceremony, award ribbons and certificates to winners, (those who place and those who participate.) Give frisbees to everyone and trophies to the winning centers. Prepare a giant banana split and let them all "have at it."

Kay McCreery, Montgomery Parks and Recreation Department, 1010 Forest Avenue, Montgomery, Alabama, 36106

HELPFUL HOMEWORK

A tutorial program conducted at the recreation center by sororities, fraternities, church groups. Center should have encyclopedias and most local schools will supply text books.

STREET - WISE

The local police and fire departments assist in making children "street-wise" through information and discussions on safety. Topics include: stranger danger, bicycle, skateboard and traffic safety, emergency phone use and fire safety. Parents are also invited to attend.

SUPER BOWL PARTY

Begin by renting a large screen TV to show the Super Bowl game. Provide refreshments and "legal" betting opportunities.

KNOTHOLE GANG CAMP SERIES

To suit the varied interests of the differing age groups, design a camp program series ranging from crafts to visual and performing arts, to just plain fun. The camp staff consists of a combination of recreation staff and visiting artists.

1) MUSICAL THEATRE CAMP -

Ages 10-13 - This camp is designed to help budding young actors and actresses develop their talents. Intense instruction will be given by qualified professionals in dance, music, and theater by qualified professionals. The camp ends with a free performance of a musical production to area playground program participants and/or family and friends.

2) VISUAL ARTS CAMP -

Ages 11-15 - This ia a camp especially suited to those "serious" young artists who wish to expand their talents. Hold classes in painting, drawing, pottery, and mixed media taught by visiting artists.

3) YOUTH CHORAL CAMP -

Ages 6-12 - This camp is for the true music lover. The classes will strengthen the musical appreciation and abilities in all the campers through reading, singing, moving to and listening of all types of music.

4) ADVENTURE CAMP-

Ages 6-9 - These exciting adventures will appeal to the young explorer. Campers will enjoy field trips to historic places and experience the great outdoors. This camp is designed as a hands-on experience in which campers will have completed projects to bring home.

Susan Britt, City of Rock Hill, Parks, Recreation and Tourism Department., SCN Center Suite 104, 100 Dave Lyle Blvd. Rock Hill, SC 29730

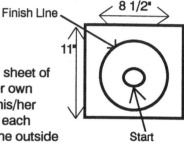

EARTHWORM RACES

Two concentric (one inside of the other) circles are drawn on an 8 1/2" x 11" sheet of paper. Each participant is given a copy of the drawing which acts as his/her own personal race course. Prior to the start of the race, each contestant places his/her earthworm within the lines/boundaries of the inside circle. At a given signal, each contestant attempts to get his/her earthworm to crawl over/past the line of the outside circle. The one to do so first is the winner.

Rules:

1) The entire earthworm must be within the lines/boundaries of the inside circle at the start of the race.
2) Contestants may not touch his/her earthworm at any time during the race. However, he/she may blow on it, tap their fingers behind, next to, or in front of the earthworm.
3) The paper must remain flat on the table/level surface at all times during the race.
4) The only restriction as to the size of the earthworm that are used, is that they must fit completely inside the lines/boundaries of the inside circle at the start of the race.

FOOD BINGO

Children love to play Bingo and love to eat. Putting them together makes for a great entertainment. Children play Bingo for an hour and then take a break to enjoy whatever snack is scheduled. The children resume playing and competing for prizes. Examples of treats are: Banana Split Bingo, Cookie Monster Bingo, Pizza Bingo, Beanie-Weenie Bingo, Beach Blanket Bingo, (kids come dressed in beach clothes, bring their beach towel to sit on and have cookout type food.)

Allen Greene, Virginia Beach Recreation Center - Bow Creek 3427 Club House Road, Virginia Beach, VA 23462

PET ROCK RACES

Part one of this event is the creation of a pet rock. Get smooth, rounded rocks and use enamel paint and permanent markers to create the rock's features. Now go to the races...the contestants take turns rolling their pet rocks down a slanted board. Each rock is timed to determine the winner.

TOO KOOL
TO
RECREATE....

TEENS

ROLLIN' THE PARK

DESCRIPTION:

This is a skateboarding event for teens. Use any large flat space (tennis courts work great) that can be roped off and controlled. Registered teens compete in three events: freestyle - use of the skateboard only (no ramps, etc.); streetstyle - use skateboard on ramps, curbs, junk cars, slide, etc.; and ramp riding - 1/2 pipe, 1/4 pipe, launch ramp, straight wall. All participants must wear helmets and knee pads!

RELATED ACTIVITIES:

Invite a professional skateboard rider to present safety talks and demonstrations. Have skateboard shop display equipment.

MATERIALS:

*Ramps, tables, chairs (for registration), cash box, change, EMS, and security (for crowd control). *Ramps can be made with the help of a local skateboard shop.

POSSIBLE RESOURCES:

Local skateboard or bike shop, radio stations, teen centers.

CREATIVE PROMOTIONS:

Go real biazzare and radical with the flyer. Distribute at bike shops, arcades, teen centers. MC for event.

JUDGING CATEGORIES:

Use skateboard and bike shop owners, or someone knowledgeable about skateboard techniques, as judges. Prizes can be donated boards, trucks, stickers, posters, and t-shirts. NO TROPHIES!

RECORD CONVENTION

Work in conjunction with a local radio station and record store to provide a time for teenagers, and adults, to buy rare and used compact discs, tapes, and records. The compact discs, tapes, and records can be brought in by various dealers. You can set up a special swap and shop area where individuals can rent a small space, for a nominal fee, to sell their old music. The record store can help you find the dealers, and the radio station will provide publicity and door prizes, such as more music and concert tickets.

ADVENTURE SUMMER CAMP

Tap on the resources in your area and offer 12-15 year olds instruction and adventures in selected activities such as scuba diving, snorkling, crabbing, deep sea fishing, ropes course, rappeling roller skating, fossil hunting, bike rides, and end the series of adventures with a group camp out.

TEEN ALL SPORTS AND CULTURAL OPPORTUNITIES

DESCRIPTION:

Sports, cultural and other enrichment activities comprise T.A.S.C.O. The program relies on interagency cooperation, as it is promoted and initiated at the community/recreation center level. T.A.S.C.O. activities are available to teens, 13-17, who are still enrolled in school. For most activities, memos asking for replies of intent to participate and/or a roster listing are sent to the centers.

SPORTS -

Flag football teams represent each center (15 man roster, limitation). Each player and coach receives a t-shirt and games are played every Saturday from 1 - 3 p.m. Upon request, the recreation department provides transportation. To end the season, plan a barbecue and awards ceremony.

Plan four field trips per year for the teens who have participated in the recreational, educational and civic activities at the center level. The recreation department can purchase tickets to a concert. Arrange a tour through the performing arts center or auditorium beforehand. Begin the night's activities with a box dinner at a park or college campus. Dinner money has been raised by the participants during funds raisers earlier in the year.

"GO FOR IT" --

Schedule two - one week teen camps, which include ecology, drama, team and creative play, arts and crafts, and field trips to local attractions. A one time registration fee covers transportation, lunch and admissison fees. Be resourceful when planning the field trips and investigate all options in your area. Possible field trips: nature centers, planetariums, art museums, state/national parks, and special tours, whenever possible. Daytime activities could include: mini-golf, a trip to the beach, sand sculpture contest, photography/scavenger hunt, roller skating, "All Sport Morning" (softball, volleyball, frisbee golf), "aqua-olympics". Sponsor a "contest" for ecology. See who can bring in the most cans during the week. Schedule an appearance/instruction from a drama teacher or mime artist. Offer improvisational acting and juggling lessons. Be sure to allow for "free time" first thing in the morning and the last thing at the end of the day (15 minutes, each). End the camp with a picnic, including volleyball games, treasure hunt and other popular activities that you have seen develop during the week.

TEEN CAMPOUTS -

Schedule T.A.S.C.O. campouts, once again, available to active participants, and offer these during the three major school breaks -- Spring, Summer, and Christmas (weather permitting). The campouts could be at a local park where activities can easily be played. Activites could include: horseshoes, volleyball, table tennis, music, flag football, manhunt, movies, campfire, marshmellow roasting, wargames, archery instruction, orienteering, hayride, night hike, pizza eating contest. Be sure to prepare an equipment and necessities list for campers.

RESOURCES:

For assistance: Coaches, sporting goods stores, local attractions, performing arts centers, auditoriums, arts council, skating rinks.

For participation: communtiy/recreation centers, student governments, teen councils, church youth groups, special interest clubs, sports club or teens.

CREATIVE PROMOTIONS:

Seek co-sponsorship with the local radio station that gears itself to teens. Produce a monthly newsletter that is sent to all the teens who have participated in the program and to the resources listed above.

JUDGING CATEGORIES:

SPORTS - Give trophies to 1st, 2nd, and 3rd place teams and 3 MVP trophies, determined by ballot.

Bob Valenti, City of St. Petersburg, Leisure Service Department/Recreation Division, P.O. Box 2842, St. Petersburg, FL 33731

AFTER PROM PARTY

Offer a safe alternative to the "normal" after prom activities by inviting high school junior and seniors to your center for an after prom party. Have the following available: D.J., movies, dance contest, video games, table games and refreshments, such as pizza and a salad bar. Award donated door prizes throughout the night. Charge a minimal admisssion.

BATTLE OF THE BRAINS

Four representatives from each area high school, comprise a team for competition for scholarship money. With the assistance of the school district, questions will be asked on subjects such as history, current issues, geography, science, literature, humanities, etc. Winning school is determined by the highest score within a half hour. Apply single elimination rules. The two top schools compete in the final round (High IQ Bowl). For scholorship money secure a local bank.

Greensboro Parks and Recreation Department, Greensboro, NC

STUPID PET TRICKS

During National Pet Week (2nd week in May) work with a mall or use a recreation center as the site for this event. Teens bring their pets in to perform their special trick(s), and the audience is the judge. Prizes could be provided by a local pet store.

BRAINY BLOWOUT

As an incentive to get and have them maintain good grades, offer the regulars at your recreation center spiffs upon receiving a 3.0 or better report card. Favorite spiffs include: concerts, pizza parties, submarine sandwiches, build your own sundae, or a trip to a popular attraction. At the end of the year offer special awards to "most improved," "best overall average," and to the oldest member who is "most likely to suceed."

OVER THE TOP ARM WRESTLING TOURNAMENT

Charge a registration fee for this double elimination event ($8.00) and designate 8 different weight classes (124 - under, 125 - 135, 136 - 154, 155 - 169, 170 - 184, 185 - 209, 210 - 224, 225 and over). Have contestants weigh in the day of the event. Get an local sporting goods store or gym to co-sponsor this event and supply the prizes. Rules and regulations: one official at each table; official starts and calls winner and makes final decision; each match has a 30 second time limit. To reduce chance of injury, second match does not immediately follow 1st match; one official time keeper for each match; wrestling table specifications: table top is 25" x 25"; height is 35", made of wood, carpet and pads; one foot has to be floor at all times; no penalties for false starts.

© Wilco

DREAM DATE COMPETITION

At one of your teen dances, Valentines, for instance, select 16 couples (from a random drawing) to compete in a contest, similiar to "The Newlywed Game." Couples have previously completed a questionnaire and must be present to win. Prepare a stage and backdrop with all the glitz of television. Four of the couples will win a chaperoned night in a stretch limosine, their choice of the menu at a popular restaurant, a concert or just cruising in the limo and a midnight snack at a place of their choice. Prepare a written schedule of plans/permission slip for parents to sign.

Bob Valenti City of St. Petersburg, Leisure Service Department/Recreation Division, P.O. Box 2842, St. Petersburg, FL 35731

LOOK AND ACT ALIKE CONTEST

Give teens the opportunity to imitate a person such as a celebrity, political figure, local personality, teacher, etc. Judge participants on detail of appearance and accuracy of personality characteristics (voice, body language, and actions).

CINDERELLA PROM

Make this dance as much like a prom as you wish -- boutonnieres, king and queen, favors. Just make sure the dress is casual.

PROFESSIONAL MODELING TECHNIQUES

Introduce teens to the world of fashion modeling by getting the cooperation of a professional modeling school to come to your center. Participants (male and female) will learn modeling techniques, personal development, make-up artistry and how to make modeling a career, if they choose to do so. End the event with a Fashion Production using the "new models," and see if the modeling school will give a scholarship to the most promising student.

BATTLE OF THE BANDS

Make a football stadium the battle field for band competition. Invite established, but non-professional, pop bands to compete for the grand prize -- a free recording session at a sound studio. Screen bands by requiring a demo tape or by holding an audition. Bands would compete in two categories: 1) original music and 2) non-original music.

TEEN OF THE MONTH

A 12th grade male and female are selected each month for their outstanding leadership, community activities, honors and scholarship. Winners receive a $100.00 scholarship from local businesses.

CROCK POT COOKING

This class is tailored especially for young adults who are acquiring the skills necessary for an independent lifestyle. Students will prepare the meal together, put it into one pot, then enjoy sampling the identical recipe that has already been cooked -- just like on TV! Kitchen safety and clean up will be emphasized.

RENT A TEEN

Recreation center prints and mails a quarterly directory listing youth who perform yard work, babysitting, housework, painting, car washing and waxing, and other domestic chores needed.

Greensboro Parks and Recreation Department Greensboro, NC

STEVE MARTIN FILM FESTIVAL

On a weekend evening(s) show a variety of movies starring this ex-Saturday Night Live funny guy, such as "The Jerk," "Dead Men Don't Wear Plaid," "Roxanne," etc. Give out door prizes between movies that deal with silly pranks.

THE GREAT ALL-NIGHTER

This is a four to five hour treasure hunt through your city that involves going from place to place searching for clues that lead to the big treasure, such as $150 or maybe two hours anywhere the winner and three friends want to go in a limousine.

GAMES OF OLD ENGLAND

Participants play either croquet or badminton. Door prizes and awards are given and tea and crumpets (iced tea and cookies) are served.

GAMES OF CHANCE

Set up a room with all the big Las Vegas style games such as, Black Jack, Roulette Wheel, Craps and Bingo. Use play money and make the odds easier to beat. At the end of the night, have a prize auction with the play money to "sell" donated prizes that are appropriate for teens.

PRETTY AS A PORTRAIT

Kids, 8 to 13 years old, learn to draw family and friends after practicing basic portrait drawing in four lessons.

SUPER SWEATSHIRT

Kids, 9 - 14 years old, bring a sweatshirt from home and decorate it with applique and paints.

MTV PARTY

To recruite teens for participation in your ongoing programs, schedule a MTV party (large screen), and while they are there, show slides or videos of past events and activities.

Here are some additional activities for teens, ranging from recreation center events to high adventure outings!

Youth Commission/Advisory Board
Battle of the Sexes Weight Control
For Fun and Profit
Photography Workshop
Teen Videos
Dance Classes
Computer Seminars
First Aid Training
Sports Programs
Sand Volleyball
Cycling Trips
Social Dance Classes
Advanced Lifesaving/WSI
Lawn Maintenance Techniques
Water Park Trips
Friday Night Videos
Road Rally and Concert
Single Parent Family Nights
Game Room
Lazar Tag Tournament
Spooks, Spares, and Strikes
Video Disc Jockey
The Sky's the Limit

Mash Day Counseling and Employment Services
Friday Night Live Exercise Classes
Whitewater Rafting
T-shirt Night
Teens on Screen
Extra Help
50s Night
Date-A-Hunk
Rocktober
Camping/Canoeing Trip
Trash Bash
New Years Eve Lock-In
Late Night Trips
Ghost Tours
Screaming Meamies
Nerds Are People, Too!
Friday Freak-Out
Floor Hockey
Live Mannequins
Patio Barbecues
VIP/Workreation
Tent Rentals
Career-Oriented Trips

YUPPIES
AND
UP....

ADULTS

ULTIMATE SCAVENGER HUNT

DESCRIPTION:

Here is a zany, yet classy, hunt where participants, 18 and over, enjoy a night on the town, riding in limousines hunting down answers and articles stated on a clue sheet. In addition to receiving a t-shirt (to be worn as the outshirt at all times during the hunt), participants receive a survival kit and Panic Package. This is not a race, but points have a numerical value and the team with the highest score wins. Limit the hunt to 2 or 3 hours, as limousine service is costly.

SCAVENGER ITEMS: 1. A yard sale sign. 2. A receipt from a parking garage dated ?/??/89. 3. A gameroom token. 4. A plastic coated paper clip. 5. A wrapped toothpick. 6. What is the name of the upcoming local theatre play? 7. How many tons of wings does a local restaurant sell? 8. At night, what colors do you see on a local hotel sign? 9. Get a souvenir from an establishment at an intersection where all of the roads change names upon crossing. 10. A McDonalds coffee stirrer. 11. A bank depsit envelope. 12. A $2.00 bill. 13. A tide or weather chart. 14 Anything with the word "your town" printed on it. 15. A dis count coupon. 16. What is the stand-up display in the lobby at your local theatre? 17. What is the name of a recently opened club or restaurant on a specific street? 18. An acorn. 19. A green apple. 20. How many tennis courts are at a local park or complex? 21. Any free newspaper. 22. An in-store promotional ad. 23. What is the date of dedication of a local park, building etc? 25. An Alaskan area code. 26. Anything with the "local mascot" on it. 27. What is the price of super unleaded gas at all three gas stations on the corner of two streets. 28. Anything with the name of the State University on it. 29 A bar of soap from a hotel or motel. 30. A brochure from the local Tourism Center.

MATERIALS:

Panic Package - (Typed this on the outside) - 25 points if you return the Panic Package unopened. Include: .25c taped to a business card of recreation supervisor saying "since you opened this envelope there must be a reason. Call me at....." Also include a requirement for a dictionary page that includes "Spheroid." (75points) and a copy of the Recreation Department brochure (50 points). The Survival Kit includes: pencil, paper, film for Instamatic, city map, plastic bags, bandages, hints, rules, clues and Panic Package.

RESOURCES:

For services and prize donations: limo services, photo shops, gyms/fitness centers, restaurants and activity centers. For participation: contact singles clubs, church groups, special interest groups.

CREATIVE PROMOTIONS:

Get co-sponsorship of radio station geared to 18 - 24 demographics and /or of a fitness center or lounge for registration distribution. Use some clues and questions similiar to those that will be asked that evening in radio spots and as lead-ins on written public service announcement.

JUDGING CATEGORIES:

Rules: 1. Actual time in Limo, 3 hours (7:30 - 1030 p.m.). 2. Any time used after 10:30 p.m. must be paid by the team. 3. You must travel as a team. All 6 members should actually get out of the limo and move around as a team. 4. You must wear the t-shirt at all times, as a top layer. 5. The list of clues are in no specific order. 6. You can only use (1) item per answer. 7. Teams are responsible to pay for any damage to the limousines or any other damage they may cause. 8. It is understood that any cost incurred for tolls, scavenger items, or other related items are at the expense of the teams. 9. The Chauffeur must not take photos or leave the limo, therefore, do not ask her/him for any help. 10. Photos taken as hunt items must include all 6 team members if specified. Print item # on the back of the photo. 11. The maximum number of photos that you may submit at the end of the evning is 21. 12. If allotted film is used up...that's all there is.. If you need more, team will have to purchase it. 13. The team is responsible for damage of cameras on loan. 14. Always rember the "SPIES." 15. In case of dire emergency..or bail is needed, call the Recreation Department at 555-1212. 16. In case of minor needs - open survival kit.

Bonnie Vaillancourt, Largo Recreation Depaartment, 65 4th Street, NW, Largo, FL 34640

ART ENCOUNTER

This affair conducts scheduled tours to homes of artists' studios and is led by professional artists, who encourage lively and active discussion.

ADULT CLASS REVIEW

DESCRIPTION:

Don't miss this opportunity to be a star. The students from all the adult classes are putting on a show in the theatre. Invite your friends and family to come see what you have learned in just 6 short weeks. Clogging, Belly Dance, Social Dance, Jazz, Tap, Ballet, and Judo are just a few of the classes that will be participating in the Review. The arts and crafts classes are also included in the Review. An exhibit area will be set up in the theatre lobby for Cake Decorating, Oil Painting, Stained Glass, Flower Arranging, Pottery, Knitting, Crochet, and Quilting exhibits and demonstrations.

RELATED ACTIVITIES:

Have a local personality or comedian to MC the Review. Provide refreshments for a reception after the Review. There is a rehearsal prior to the big show.

MATERIALS:

Audio-visual equipment, microphone, record players, recording equipment, lights, and sound equipment, spotlight, and food service supplies.

POSSIBLE RESOURCES:

Local comedian for the MC, or ask a radio or television personality.

CREATIVE PROMOTIONS:

Word of mouth through the adult class program is the most successful way to advertise this event. A flier is distrubuted to the instuctors and students.

Janis C. Prock, Virginia Beach Parks and Recreation Department, 800 Monmouth Lane, Virginia Beach, Virginia 23464

ALL NIGHT CERAMICS

Offer a night time ceramics session with maximum enjoyment. Each participant brings a covered dish or snack item to munch on during the evening while finishing their ceramic pieces. Optional: Charge a fee ($2.00 - $3.00)

PHOTOGRAPHY SCAVENGER HUNT

Give participants a list of things to photograph (policeman blowing a bubble, fireman polishing a fire engine) and a deadline for entries. Sponsor in conjuction with a newspaper or television station. Use the 12 best photographs to compile, then sell, a calendar.

CEMETERY WALKING TOUR

Let your city's past "come alive" as a walking tour through the cemetery reveals the burial places of prominent people from the social, political, and architectural history of the area.

SAMPLE SALE

DESCRIPTION:
This is a great event in which to get local businesses and agencies involved. Each business pays a set fee for a booth at the Sample Sale. They then set up a booth with information regarding their business, community service...etc. They also bring printed promotional items (i.e. key chains, memo pads, pens, coasters, frisbees, etc.) on which their name and logo is printed. An admission fee of $2.00 - $5.00 is then charged to people interested in attending the Sample Sale. Participants visit the different booths and have a chance to talk with the local business owners and administrators. Local residents have the opportunity to learn just what all is available to them in their community. At the same time, participants leave with many different free "gadgets" that they have collected throughout the day.

RELATED ACTIVITIES:
Have local businesses donate prizes to be raffled off throughout the day. Have a large area for local businesses and artists to display samples of their product or work.

MATERIALS:
Indoor or outdoor facility large enough to accomodate all of the booths, tables for each booth (optional), paint/chalk to mark off each booth, PA system, music, cash box.

POSSIBLE RESOURCES:
Chamber of Commerce, local civic organizations, homeowners, clubs, Boy Scouts, Girl Scouts, church groups, businesses, hospitals, banks.

CREATIVE PROMOTIONS:
Flyers made in the shape of a giant "sale" price tag.

NORMAN'S POOL PARTY

My friend called and asked me to come to his Fourth of July Pool Party. I said, "Norman, do you have a pool ?" Norman said, "No, everyone is bringing their own rubber pool." What great fun on a hot summer day!

SCHOOL- WIDE REUNION

People might know what a lot of their graduating classmates are doing, because they get together for class reunions, but what about those friends and acquaintances that were upper or lower classmen? Plan an annual "Jonesville" High School Reunion for every and anyone who has ever attended Jonesville and schedule it the same weekend every year. It will catch on. Begin by accumulating each classes' reunion mailing list. (This could be a great money maker.)

COOKING CLASS IDEAS

Schedule cooking classes to reflect current "food fads" and/or a unique experience, such as an afternoon tea.

FAJITAS -
Learn how to prepare fajita meat, pico de gallo, and guacamole. This could be taught by a chef from a local Mexican restaurant.

HELPFUL HINTS FOR HERBS -
This course deals with"everything" regarding herbs, including the growing, cooking and uses in teas, butter, landscaping, and dried flowers.

AFTERNOON TEA -
Contract a British "born and breed" to discuss the traditions and types of tea used in the Mother Country. Serving tea and appropriate food items will be discussed and sampled. Learn the difference of tea time and "high tea."

VEGETARIAN MEALS IN MINUTES -
Learn to easily incorporate delicious natural and healthy vegetarian cooking into your daily meals. Participants prepare and sample a variety of natural foods and beverages.

TERRIFIC TORTELLINI -
Contract an Italian chef to acquaint cooking students with tortellini and its several variations, plus sauces, spices and creative uses.

SOCK HOP

Return to the days of yesteryear -- the Fifties. Dress in creative Fifties "threads" (that would be "neat-o") and have a costume contest. Other contests could include the jitterbug, hula hoop, hair style (men and women) and lip sync. Limit group in lip sync to five and be sure to award "unbelievably cool" prizes: better than the "Book of Love;" better than "Love Potion Number Nine," even better than a pair of "Blue Suede Shoes." Offer food such as hot dogs, hamburgers, chips and bowls of bubble gum and candy bars. Decorate the building to depict a gym. To kick off the event, stage a car show cruise on a designated route.

INSOMNIACS TOUR

DESCRIPTION:
Do you get your "second wind" around midnight, or do you work the "night shift?" If so, this trip is just for you! The bus will depart at 1:00 a.m. and will return at 6:00 a.m. We'll take a fun look at "life after dark" in the city. The tour may include a lounge, bakery, newspaper, bus station, police station, hospital and post office. The trip will end at sunrise with a catered gourmet breakfast.

ACTIVITIES:
Experience the twightlight shift of a local bank, find out what happens to buses after their last run of the day. Visit McDonalds, a planetarium, or movie theater (special showing of current movie).

RESOURCES:
Industries with night shift employees, hospitals, utility company employees, senior citizens.

CREATIVE PROMOTIONS:
Flyers and posters in 24 hour stores and at companies with three shifts.

THE WORLD'S LARGEST...

In Greenville, SC, the Hyatt Hotel and the Greenville Zoo host "The World's Largest Office Party" (Media celebrities and other dignitaries are the bartenders and vie to see who can get the most tips. The "loser" gets to clean out the zoo's elephant pen). Proceeds go to the Greenville Zoo. In Broward County, in Florida, a 700 foot barbecue grills cooks over 50,000 chicken halves for the "World's Largest Barbecue." Amenities include live bands, organized sports, arts and crafts show, classic car show, hot air balloons, petting zoo, all the food, desserts and soft drinks you can consume -- all for $12.00 (Children under 9, free). The proceeds go to the Lukemia Society and major sponsors include a radio station, a chicken company, beer company, soft drink company, and a yogurt franchise. Host your own "World's Largest,..." by using available resources in your area.

SECRETARIES OLYMPICS

DESCRIPTION:

Here's a great event for all the secretaries in the world! This event is most appropriate for National Secretaries Week. There are a couple different ways to set up a Secretaries Olympics -- either at individual offices or at a central location. Secretaries or teams perform clerical tasks and are judged on skill and/or within time limitations.

ACTIVITIES:

Activities can include: paper wad basketball throw; take a grossly mis spelled paragraph and make corrections; string 20 paperclips together, then take apart; prepare a cup of coffee -- with cream and sugar -- and deliver to "the boss;" unstaple 50 staples; change toner in copy machine; filing; word scramble (alphabetize a list of words); stapling accuracy (draw circles on the left hand top corner of a stack of 20 sheets of paper, and contestants are judged on how many circles they staple within 30 seconds.

MATERIALS:

Paper, wastebaskets, typewriters, paperclips, coffee makers, coffee, cream, sugar, staplers, staples, copy machine, toner refills, stapler removers.

RESOURCES:

Corporations, banks and office complexes for contestants. Ask a radio station to be a sponsor, and then the contestants would call the radio stations with their times for each event, and the station announces the winners throughout the day. A radio station could also provide a remote if the competition is at a central location.

CREATIVE PROMOTIONS:

Send invitations out to corporations in the form of a giant memo to the secretaries.

COMMUNITY GARDENS CONTEST

Contestants have their front and back yards judged in the following categories: smallest and largest garden, best shade garden, best wildflower garden, best experimental garden, best flower garden, largest variety in a flower garden, best use of sculpture in a garden, best overall garden.

HARVEST MOON BALL

Rather than dance under the stars, dance in them, on top of a mountain. Participants meet in a parking lot and board a chartered bus, complete with hors d'oeuvres, champagne, and music. The bus arrives on top of the mountain where the dance is held. Include soft lights, chinese lanterns and a live band.

Adults enjoy learning and participating in a variety of classes, such as the following:

ADULT CLASSES:

Left Handed Affair In The Square
Small Business Management
Arm Chair Travel
Japanese Culture
Water Aerobics
Low Cholesterol/Healthy Heart Cooking

Sign Language
Crystals
Local Tours
Who Are Those Strangers In You Dreams?
Improving Your Memory

GARDENING CLASSES:
How Not To Kill Your Houseplants
Selecting and Planting Bulbs For Spring Color
Planting A Fall Garden
Design Your Garden With Low Maintenance
Square Foot Gardening

ARTS AND CRAFTS:

Stained Glass
Spanish Moss Wreath
Calligraphy
English Smocking
Pineneedle Baskets

Wheat Weaving
Bread Making
Bird Feeder Workshop
Cartooning

OFF THE
ROCKER....

SENIORS

SENIOR CITIZEN J.O.Y (JUST OLDER YOUTH) DAY
"SPRING J.O.Y. DAY"

DESCRIPTION:

This special event is designed to provide senior citizens and their guests with a day of entertainment, fellowship, information and referrals. Each senior citizen's center and senior citizens club are asked to submit one act of entertainment in either singing, dancing, comedy or music. Also, letters are mailed to all agencies involved with the elderly, asking if they would like to reserve space and exhibit information pertaining to the elderly, (such as Social Security, Legal Aid, Social Services, Housing, etc.) Lunch can either be a bag lunch brought by those in attendance or through a restaurant donation. Coffee and doughnuts can also be donated for breakfast.

RELATED ACTIVITIES:

Provided entertainment in dancing, singing, piano medleys and comedy.

MATERIALS:

Program, PA system, cue cards for M.C., oldest senior award (this award is presented to the oldest senior male and the oldest senior female during the program). Vehicles for limited transporation.

POSSIBLE RESOURCES:

Participants usually come from nursing homes, day care centers, senior centers, individual citizens.

CREATIVE PROMOTIONS:

Through senior citizen's newsletter, news media, T.V., letters or invitations.

Gloria Alley, Recreation Supervisor, Virginia Beach Department of Parks and Recreation, 4700 Recreation Drive, Virginia Beach, VA 23456

MOM, POP AND THE KIDS

Seniors invite the youth to their facility to teach them about the "good ole' days" and about the current lives of the older citizens. Activities include dancing, relays, storytelling and travel slide presentations.

SENIOR VOLLEYBALL TOURNAMENT

Use a balloon as the volleyball. Participants stay seated but follow regular volleyball game procedures.

ROARING 20'S PARTY

Decorate the building in the decor of a night club; provide period music, including the Charleston, so the seniors can kick it up. Include a costume and hair style contest, since everyone will be dressed in 1920's attire.

CAMP SENIORITY

DESCRIPTION:

This is a day camp for seniors -- a great opportunity for fun and games for senior adults 55 and over. Schedule this two week affair (3 - 4 days of each week) during the milder weather -- spring or fall - and charge a one time fee ($35.00 for 1 week and $65.00 for both weeks). Lunch is included in the fee. Have scholarships for persons unable to pay. Events include leisure activities such as day trips to local interest sites and businesses, entertainment, arts and crafts, guest speakers and non-strenuous sports activities. Give participants a choice between two activities at any given time. Activities could include: Trips to a local radio or television station, city hall, county court house, newspaper office, brewery, winery, planetarium, art museum, zoo, park. Use a van or bus to transport seniors to a state park, a university, whitewater rafting, retirement village, nearby area of interest. Sports activities: Begin each day with a half hour of warming-up exercise and a short walk, then offer any of the following throughout the day: putt-putt, shuffleboard, tennis, bicycles, nature walk, horseshoes, golf instruction, horseback riding. Offer ongoing craft classes taught by fellow seniors. Other activities could include a scavenger hunt (in the neighborhood or in the woods), cooking classes (stir-fry, low fats, ice cream making). Entertainment and enrichment - invite the following speakers in for educational sessions: mechanic, landscaper/ horticulturalist, nutritionalist, Highway Patrolmen (defense driving) traveloque, representative from Council of Aging, AARP, skin care product, American Cancer Society, American Heart Association, HOSPICE, doctors, chiropractors, hospital.

MATERIALS:

Vans and/or buses, sports equipment, arts and crafts supplies, medical forms with doctor's permission to include history and medications.

RESOURCES:

Local and area senior programs, recreation department, Council on Aging.

CREATIVE PROMOTIONS:

AARP, seniors newsletters, registration forms, posters, mailing list. Sell camp sovenirs such as tote bags, visors, t-shirts, all reading "We Go Over 55."

Jan Bankhead, City of Greenville Parks and Recreation Departments, 200 Park Drive, Greenville, SC 29601

HOE DOWN FOR SENIORS

Seniors dress in western attire and join in on square dancing, pony rides, horseshoes, a pot luck dinner and the most favorite of all -- a pie judging contest.

SENIOR FASHION SHOW

Local department stores loan the merchandise to the women and men models for an entertaining day of fashion.

SENIOR SPORTS CLASSIC

DESCRIPTION:

A senior sports classic event will maintain and improve the health and wellness of your older adults and provide a competitive athletic and recreational experience that focuses attention on the importance of regular exercise in every individual's personal plan of health. This quality recreation experience for adults 55 and over can be administered solely on a local level, or it can serve to qualify the participants for competition on a state level where the event can be sauctioned by the U.S. National Senior Olympics. Age groups are 55-59, 60-64, 65-69, 70-74, 75 and over. Events for a sanctioned event include: swimming (goverened by U.S. Masters rules), badminton (U.S. Badminton Association), basketball free throw, cycling, pocket billiards, 10 pen bowling, eighteen "hoop" frisbee golf course, 18 hole golf tournament, horseshoes, racquetball, softball throw (distance and accuracy), table tennis (USTA Tennis), track and field, walk for fun and time, putt-putt golf, volleyball team, softball team and spin casting, for accuracy.

RELATED ACTIVITIES:

Invite other senior groups to entertain, such as square dancers, cloggers, bands, choral, kitchen bands. Arts and crafts show and sale and bake offs add to the day. Awards banquet and dance/social folllow events.

MATERIALS:

T-shirt for each participant, certificates of participation medals, specific event supplies, event numbers for each participant. Particpants provide their own equipment for events entered. Registration brochure to include liability waiver.

RESOURCES:

State college for host, so participants can stay in dormitories, Governors Council on Physical Fitness, Commission on Aging. Endorsements: AARP, USTA, American Bowling Congress. For participants: AARP newsletter, local sports associations, senior centers, area recreation departments.

Florence Recreation Division, P.O. Box 1476, Florence, SC 29503

FINANCIAL PLANNING

DESCRIPTION:

Bring in local experts to lead series of local workshops held concurrently. Participants select which to attend and switch after specifed amount of time. Topics include: 1. Wills, 2. Estate Planning, 3. Tax Preparation, 4. Planning for Retirement, 5. Planning for Children's College Education, 6. What If He Dies First?, 7. Adequate Insurance/Disability, 8. Budgeting For Today and Tomorrow, and 9. Investments.

MATERIALS:

Easel, overhead projector, calculators, magic markers.

RESOURCES:

Accountants, lawyers, professors, stock brockers, financial planners.

CREATIVE PROMOTIONS:

Posters in grocery stores, banks, senior citizens centers, women's professsional organization, civic or garden clubs, library.

CATHEDRAL TOUR

For a different senior activity, plan a tour of local cathedrals, churches and chapels, which are homes for some of the most interesting and beautiful architecture. Have a local historian or knowledgeable architect to meet you for a brief interpretation. Plan on a lunch stop to break up the day.

MYSTERY TRIP

Many times seniors don't care where they go; they just like to take trips. So, plan a trip that has a totally surprise location. Provide a quality tour and good food.

MASQUERADE MADNESS

It's ghouling good fun for the seniors at the masquerade madness. Include the usual costume contest, dancing, refreshments and games suited "just for the seniors." A favorite activity is the Crafty Pumpkin Draw, where each table has a pumpkin, glue and 5 paper bags with each containing a different item. One bag may have Q-tips, another beans, another with styrofoam peanuts, one with yarn, and one with buttons. The recreation leader directs the group to choose one of the sealed bags and next directs the group where to use that item on the pumpkin. (i.e. whatever bag the "team" chooses first will be what they use to compose the hair.) Then they choose a second bag (upon direction of the leader) and glue that item on the place announced, such as eyes. All pumpkins will be very different from one another and will make an interesting display at City Hall, a mall or at your center.

SENIOR SHENANIGANS

DESCRIPTION:

Introduce seniors to the many opportunities available at your state parks through a series of special weekends called Senior Shenanigans. This requires extensive coordination with the desired state parks in regard to reservations and any special activities you want to schedule during any one Shenanigan. Designate, for instance, six state parks which offer a variety of activites and are located near other attractions in your state. Arrange at least one of the Shenanigans to take place at a park that has scheduled a festival during that time. Each park is responsible for taking reservations. You might want to schedule some parks for 2 or 3 different times throughout the year.

RELATED ACTIVITIES:

Seek state parks with facilities for playing golf and tennis; that have hiking trails, boat cruises, lakes for fishing; and have space for dancing and playing cards. Focus one of the shenanigans around arts and crafts and have several of the seniors teach their craft(s) to the others. Arrange tours of the immediate area and provide information on the attractions in the area. One senior shenanigan could be a senior prom; a formal dance.

POSSIBLE RESOURCES:

For Assistance: State park districts and Chamber of Commerces: For Participation: Local senior organizations, AARP newsletter, other recreation agencies, libraries, State Welcome Centers.

CREATIVE PROMOTIONS:

Prepare a detailed brochure with locations, dates, prices, activities, meeting times, and deadlines for reservations. Distribute on local and state level.

Dare Bible, Tennessee State Parks, 701 Broadway, Nashville, TN 37203

SENIOR SMILES

Grab a 35mm camera and slide film. Set up an attractive backdrop (including plants) and invite the seniors to drop in for a photo session. Schedule a second get together for a slide presentation and the opportunity for the seniors to order the photographs. Each photograph is given a number, and as the slide comes up, the number is announced. Seniors make their choices and you order the prints for them to send relatives and friends. The photo session could be held during a formal or semi-formal affair.

BRIDGE BENEFIT

Designate the beneficiary and then advertise your Bridge Benefit. Charge $5.00 per person to participate. In addition to the anticipation of being the overall winning table, all those who have paid for chances for the door prizes could have their name called as a winner anytime during the benefit. Have the prizes displayed, when the players arrive; sell 25 cents chances, and when their name is called, let them choose from the prize from the table. Secure donations from banks (key chains, umbrellas, calendars), restaurants (diners for two), nurseries (plants), and from other seniors (crafts, household accessories). Save the four best prizes for the winning table. Offer players a soup and salad or sandwich lunch. Materials include door prizes, card tables and chairs, scorepads, cards, numbered tickets, pencils, beverages and lunch.

Jan Bankhead, City of Greenville Parks and Recreation Departments, 100 East Park Avenue, Greenville, SC 29601.

MILE STEPPERS

All members of the Recreation Complex who are 55 or older may participate in this walking program. Participants record all distances walked at the center and a chart is kept plotting each participants' mileage. A prize is awarded each month for the most miles walked. In addition, an exercise class for senior citizens is held 3 days a week and followed by a covered dish lunch.

BLAST INTO THE PAST

Have seniors bring a grandchild or young friend to play the "Oldies but Goodies" style games and activities that grandma and grandpa used to play.

DRAG AND BRAG DAY

Provide a day of enjoyment and reminiscing for your Seniors. Have them bring in their favorite handmade crafts to share and talk about.

HOME WITH HEART DAY

This is exercise for nursing home residents which includes - walking, rocking in rocking chairs or rolling in wheelchairs.

WINE TASTING

Have a local wine shop donate the wine and the "resident" wine stewart. Decorate the room and play classical music in the background. Have seniors wear suits and ties and formal dresses for the occasion. Offer cheese, crackers, and fruits, in addition to the wine.

HEARTY PARTY

Here's a day of fun, fitness, and games for seniors to enjoy around Valentine's Day. Begin the day with "Heart and Sole" (a health walk) and offer a variety of activities throughout the day: "Red and White List" - Within a time limit, each team compiles a list of objects that are always red and white (exit signs, American Red Cross, Coke can, candy canes); "Heartiest Laugh Contest;" "Sing Down" - use songs with words such as "hearts," "red," "honey," "kiss," "love;" "Giant Valentine" - each group decorates a giant heart with various craft supplies and scraps. The hearts are then hung for decorations for the senior dance.

MATCHMAKER

Recreation Center prints and mails a directory which lists seniors over 50 who are great at "Around the House" jobs (ironing, alterations, babysitting, housesitting, carpentry, plumbing, painting, repairs.) The directory is available to public who can then call on these seniors for assistance.

MEDIA DAY

Spend a day touring local newspaper office, radio station, TV studio. Seniors love to meet their favorite local media personalities.

SAY I DO AGAIN

Married couples repeat their vows at a mass wedding performed by a Rabbi, Priest, and Protestant minister who have worked together to prepare the ceromony. Afterwards the "newlyweds" dance to "Big Band" sounds and eat wedding cake.

THE
WHOLE GANG....

FAMILY

VOLKSWAGEN BEAUTY CONTEST

DESCRIPTION:

So...you think you have a groovy Volkswagen?!? Volkswagen owners are some of the proudest people around, and a competitive event giving them an opportunity to display their "love bug" and various models will be pleasing to their ears. Give them time to prepare, though -- at least 6 months, and go for corporate sponsorship on this one, in hopes of the grand prize winner receiving a new Volkswagen, a restored "bug" or even a trip for two to Germany. A radio station or Volkswagen dealership would be your best bet, or a cooperative effort between the three of you. Cars could be on display at the car dealership, with the dealership offering a free drawing for a car at the end of the week. Eligible people would be those who came to see the car entries.

RELATED ACTIVITES:

Schedule a public awards dinner or picnic with a German flair to announce winners. Preceed with a parade of the entries.

MATERIALS:

Registration forms, flyers, posters, prizes, p.a. system, tents, stage.

POSSIBLE RESOURCES:

Volkswagen dealerships throughout region, radio stations, travel agencies, Volkswagen and import repair shops and parts shops.

CREATIVE PROMOTIONS:

Six months prior to event decorate a Volkswagen to advertise. Display the car at various malls. Enter cars in area parades. Get firm co-sponsorship commitment from a radio station.

City of Greenville Parks and Recreation Departments, 103 Cleveland Park Drive, Greenville, SC 29601

GREAT TEXAS STEAK OUT

DESCRIPTION:

Come and have a big time at the Great Texas Steak Out where everything is REALLY BIG! Using a western theme, include a big dinner with lots of big food, contests, games, and entertainment. Big food could include 1/2 pound hamburgers or 20 ounce steak (bring your own steak or buy tickets in advance), jumbo baked potatoes, huge dill pickles, and giant glasses of iced tea.

ACTIVITIES:

Contest: chili cookoff, hog calling, log rolling, log splitting, silver dollar pitching, 10 gallon hat contest, watermelon seed spitting contest, wood carving contest, lasso instruction and competition. Games: ring toss, using hula hoops for rings, goofy golf using jumbo golf clubs (see Jolly Green Giant Day, page 21). Entertainment: 55 gallon drum bucking bronco ride (25 gallon for the kids), kiddie ride that looks like an oil rig, hayride, country dancing (clogging, square dancing, Texas Two-Step).

MATERIALS:

Grills, charcoal, matches, lighter fluid, cooking utensils, selected foods and condiments, logs, axes, silver dollars, watermelons, hula-hoops, stakes, wood blocks, jumbo golf, 55 and 25 gallon drums, stage and dance floor.

© Wilco

SUNDAY SPECTACULAR

DESCRIPTION:

This event is one remedy for those cool months of January, February and March. Plan special events that the entire family can enjoy on Sundays, such as the following, which were quoted from a promotional brochure:

"TALK TO THE ANIMALS" -

Attention animal lovers! This is the day you've all been waiting for. Walt Disney's "Jungle Book" will be shown at 2:00 p.m. Admisssion is free and everyone will be eligible to win a stuffed animal from the Stuffed Menagerie. During intermission, the City Zoo will be on hand with a snake, ferret, hedgehog, chinchilla, etc. A special prize will be given to everyone under 10 who brings a stuffed animal from home. This promises to be a day of fun for everyone.

"SPORTS SPECTACULAR" -

Basketball, karate, baseball, running, soccer, exhibits, demonstrations, displays, and much more! Find out what sports are available in your area for participation or for watching. See the latest in sports clothes, a karate demonstration; pick up schedules and information from area teams, and meet some of our area's sports figures.

"SONG AND DANCE" -

Come on out to the Playhouse and enjoy an afternoon of "song and dance." The Repertoire Company, a product of the Public School, Gifted and Talented Program will be performing. The program will be a musical revue with tunes that will be recognized by all ages.

"COLD WEATHER CRAFTS" -

What would be better than to spend a cold dreary Sunday learning new craft techniques and spreading cheer? Two new craft items will be taught. Call for reservations and items needed for class. Hot chocolate and cookies will be provided.

"ANNUAL DOLL AND TOY SHOW" -

Join local clubs, private collectors and businesses who will be showing and selling their precious collections. If you have dolls or toys to show off, contact the Recreation Department.

MATERIALS:

Materials vary with each event. Movies - large screen, video or film, chairs, prizes, refreshments; Sports- tables, chairs, refreshments, Craft - basics, such as, scissors, rulers, glue, (participants bring own materials).

POSSIBLE RESOURCES:

Talk to the Animals - Zoo, humane society. Sports - clubs (running, bicycle, swim), fitness centers, karate organizations, other recreation organizations such as the YMCA, YWCA. Song Dance - Gifted children, dance studios, theatre groups. Craft - instructors or staff. Doll and Toy Show - collectors, clubs.

CREATIVE PROMOTIONS:

Coupon Book with each page representing a different Sunday and activity. Keep a chart with attendance figures per family.

Carolee VanHorn, Recreation Supervisor, Virginia Beach Department of Parks and Recreation, 800 Monmouth Lane, Virginia Beach, Virginia 23464

OFF TO THE RACES

DESCRIPTION:

A mock Horse Race at your local park (track). Six stick horses compete to the finish line for each scheduled race. Six races are suggested for this forty-five minute event. The event announcer chooses six jockeys from those children, teens or adults standing around the track. Each jockey will wear a particular hat and bear the name appropriate for the hat. For example: male- Sammy "Sailor" (sailor's hat) or female-Sally "Sailor" (sailor's hat), male- Freddie "Fireman" (fireman's hat) or female- Franny "Fireman", etc. While the jockeys are preparing themselves for the big race, the spectators are handed one piece of special track money to bet on the jockey and horse. There will be six plastic jugs marked for each horse. Spectators are to write their name on each half of the play money and use one half to bet on the jockey and horse to "win." Provide track money in different colors for each race. At the sound of the tape, the process is to move the jockeys and horses forward by rolling of large dice. For example: six is rolled, jockey standing on six moves forward one space on a grid. What makes the race exciting is the way the announcer describes the advancement of the horses while the jockey's ad lib their role.

RELATED ACTIVITIES:

Diaper Derby (see page 59), Kiddie Karnival, Climb the Greasy Pole and family style races and entertainment for a large park festival.

MATERIALS:

Six stick horses, six occupational hats for jockeys, large dice, six-five gallon jugs, public address system, tape deck, horse race music "jockey up," race money, and three types of prizes.

POSSIBLE RESOURCES:

Participants usually come from the crowd standing around the game area.

Judith L. Wilder, Virginia Beach Department of Parks and Recreation, 470 Recreation Drive, Virginia Beach, VA 23456

GO FLY A KITE AND KITE MAKING WORKSHOP

DESCRIPTION:

The sky is the only limit when planning a kite flying contest Participants of any age bring their favorite kite or one they make at the kite making workshops -see related activities. and compete for various prizes. RULES: All kites must fly at least 2 minute; contestants will have 5 minutes to get their kite airborne; smallest kite must fly under its own power with at least 15 feet of string out, and not from being pulled.

RELATED ACTIVITIES:

Kite making workshop conducted by area instructor; hot air balloon offering tethered rides; kite and wind sock display and sales booth.

MATERIALS:

Contest: Stop watch, score sheets, wind, prizes. Workshop: Paper, string, tissue, wooden dowels, cloth, glue.

POSSIBLE RESOURCES:

Local hobby shop, kite shop for prizes.

CREATIVE PROMOTIONS:

Kite-shaped flier hanging from ceiling when/where possible.

JUDGING CATEGORIES:

Most unusual, smallest, longest tail,, largest kite, kite with most string out, oldest kite, youngest kite flyer, oldest kite flyer, most colorful, best trick kite.

A STAR IS BORN

DESCRIPTION:

Take a look at your favorite constellations and see how stars are born. Schedule this series around peak star gazing times. Each session begins with history, facts, and location of the constellations and planets to be observed that night. The expert conducting the series decides on the star gazing locations (planetarium, athletic fields, mountain top, other open spaces). Since stars are predictable and the weather is not, the instructor should keep the recreation department informed as to location(s) dates, and times.

RELATED ACTIVITIES:

Videos on astronomy; closed circuit television (at planetarium), which provides dramatic views of the moon, planets, and distant galaxies, as seen through a 20 inch telescope.

MATERIALS:

Constellation charts, telescopes.

POSSIBLE RESOURCES:

Astronomy Club, Planetarium staff, college professors.

CREATIVE PROMOTIONS:

Information sent through middle and high schools; newspaper, department fliers.

FAMILY ROAD RALLYE

DESCRIPTION:

Start your engines, and ...you're off! It's time to fill up the gas tank and call on all the relatives to join in on all the fun...the more the merrier. This event resembles a giant scavenger hunt, using your car. During a family road rallye participants attempt to follow crazy directions and clues that take them on a "leisurely drive" through the town and country. At the same time, not only must they keep their cars "on course", but they must attempt to correctly answer all the questions found in their race packets. A list of items to be collected, for example: 5 dandelions, 2 napkins from McDonalds, 3 pieces of litter from Main St..etc., is also included. Once the rallye course has been set up, the number of minutes and miles required to properly complete the course is determined. The participant's scores are then calculated, based on these figures. The object of the rallye is to keep the teams score at zero or as close to the estimated time and mileage with the least amount of mistakes. Each car/team begins the rally with a score of zero. For every minute or mile that a car comes in UNDER the estimated time and mileage, four points are added to its score. This would indicate that they have gone over the speed limit. For every minute or mile OVER the estimated figures, two points are added to its score. Ten points are added to the score for every wrong or unanswered question and for each item that was not collected.

MATERIALS:

Race course directions and clues, tabulating sheets for outgoing and incoming times and mileage for each car, watch/clock, white shoe polish to number each car's inside windshield, noisemakers to hand out to each child BEFORE they get in their parents cars and start the race, and prizes which could include car wax, windshield washer liquid, whitewall tire cleaner.

POSSIBLE RESOURCES:

Rallyes are good for competition among local businesses, fraternity and sorority groups and civic organizations. Local car dealerships, auto clubs, and CB clubs in your area.

Charlotte Parks and Recreation Departments, 600 E. 4th Street, Charlotte, N.C. 2820

SNOW DAY

DESCRIPTION:

"Snow Day" is a unique extravaganza that allows children of southern states to have a snowy, wintry experience. For many youngsters, "Snow Day" is the first experience of snow. Thanks to the processing of 40,000 lbs of ice, children can play on a "Snow Mountain" right in their own local park. Contact an ice company and make sure they can convert ice into autheutic looking snow. The process of converting 300 lbs blocks of ice to snow takes approximately 45 minutes for 40,000 lbs. (Ice blocks are granulated, then blown through a large hose to make the wire circumscribe the snowpile, allowing an apron of space between the snow and the fence all around.

RELATED ACTIVITIES:

Santa Claus is a must. A spectacular entrance, such as by helicopter or fire engine, is popular. Designate an area inside or outside - for photos with Santa. Include music, concessions, gift shops, special t-shirts.

RESOURCES:

For assistance: ice company, fire department, local weatherman.

CREATIVE PROMOTIONS:

Contact meteorologists and inform them of the event and they will play it up.

North Miami Beach Parks & Recreation Department, 17011 NE 19 Avenue, North Miami Beach, FL 33162

BiKE HIKE

DESCRIPTION:

A bike hike is an excellent family event, as it is billed as a "non-competitive, leisurely, ride" through the city or country. Offer a five, ten and twenty mile route. All pre-registered participants receive t-shirts and event packet which includes route map and coupons from restaurants, bike shops and fitness related agencies. Water, lemonade, cookies or fruit are provided throughout the course.

RELATED EVENTS:

A qualified cyclist provides safety tips and equipment, along with riding tips. BMX demonstrations can be held. The lead rider could be from the local bike club or perhaps a unicyclist leading for added "color." A local DJ serves as master of ceremonies and provides the remote with music. Ask the local bike shops to set up a table to display bike assessories and safety equipment.

MATERIALS:

Registration forms, pencils, event packets, water, lemonade, cups, cookies, fruit, tables, chairs, PA system, First Aid kit, sag wagon.

CREATIVE PROMOTIONS:

By involving a local DJ and asking him to be the MC, you will naturally get good pre-event coverage. Calls into the radio station are very effective. Have local newspaper sponsor event (name event after them), and run 1/2 page ads in paper for FREE.

A bike shop often donates a 10-speed for a drawing at the beginning of the event. A safety packet is also a good give away and includes: helmet, gloves, refelective strips, water bottle and cage, etc. Have two give-a-ways: 1 for adults, 1 for children.

City of Greenville Parks and Recreation Departments, 103 Cleveland Park Drive, Greenville, SC 29601

FAMILY REUNION DAY

DESCRIPTION:

Calling all three generations...pack an "old-fashioned" summertime picnic lunch and come out to enjoy this entire day of crazy "family-oriented" contests. Get your entire family together and come out to cheer one another on as they compete for fun and prizes. The day will begin with the extremely entertaining diaper derby where babies, 2 years and younger, will compete in several different categories. The second event of the day will be the Grandmother's Beauty Contest for grandmothers 40 years and younger. The last event, which will wind-up this day of family fun will be a Grandfather's Crazy Tie contest. Don't forget your cameras, VCR's, plenty of film, and a comfortable blanket to sit on.

RELATED ACTIVITIES:

Have families bring photo albums, slides, movies and videos and present on a giant movie screen made of white painted plywood; outdoor scavenger hunt... Families vs. families. Have a professional photographer taking family portraits..one crazy portrait and one serious portrait. Have a parade of "mini floats," which are decorated red wagons. Play "giant monopoly," which is a monopoly game set up using all of the squares of a residential block.

MATERIALS:

Stage, PA system, participant badges, prizes, measuring tape, start and finish line for rattle race, or start the babies in the center of a parachute which is spread out on the ground.

POSSIBLE RESOURCES:

Baby products companies. Pediatricians as the judges. Local doctors' office (obstetricians), nursery schools, hospitals, senior citizen clubs. Local diaper cleaning/laundry services. Baby Talk magazine.

CREATIVE PROMOTIONS:

Flyers cut in the shape of a diaper, giant diaper pin, bow tie...etc.

JUDGING CATEGORIES:

Diaper Derby - chubbiest cheeks, most hair, least hair, biggest eyes, most uniquely dressed, rattle race, parent-child look-alike, curliest hair. Grandmother's Beauty Contest - Most grandchildren, most great grandchildren, youngest, oldest, shortest, tallest, born furthest away, best smile, best talent, most unique talent, nicest walk/poise, most beautiful. Grandfather's Crazy Tie Contest - Most colorful, most unique, longest, shortest, boldest, oldest, thinest, widest, best western tie, best bow tie, brightest, nicest formal tie.

City of Charlotte Parks and Recreation Departments, 600 East Fourth Street, Charlotte, NC 28202-2864

DADDY-DAUGHTER DANCE

DESCRIPTION:

Make this Valentine's Day a special one by celebrating it with someone special...your Dad. We cordially invite you to join us for a delightful evening filled with music, dancing, contest, raffles, and a four course catered dinner.

RELATED ACTIVITIES:

Each year have a different theme for the dance; i.e. Hawaiian Lua, Country Western Hoedown, Sock Hop, etc.

MATERIALS:

Valentine decorations, PA System, disc jockey, backdrop for portraits, corsages, games, prizes, camera film, batteries, photographer, refreshments, "build your own sundae" supplies, catered dinner, raffle tickets.

POSSIBLE RESOURCES:

Local photographer, florist, schools, church you groups, Brownie troops.

SEA TURTLE RACES

DESCRIPTION:

This is an individual event that requires 5 people (or more) to compete by racing their cardboard turtles to the finish line. The turtles are attached to a wooden fixture by a cord approximately 15 feet long. Each turtle has its name printed on it but the name does not reflect how the turtle will perform in the race. The announcer gives each group of contestants specific instructions on how to make the turtle advance forward by pulling gently on the cord. Everyone is given a few moments to practice. To start the race, each turtle is placed flat on the ground with head pointing to contestants at the base of the rig. On the signal begin the walking procedure. (Walking procedure: turtle will "walk" toward player by player pulling gently on the cord, thereby lifting the head and body. Repeated lifting and relaxing "walks" the turtle to the finish line.) Jerking on the cord or excited play causes the turtle to lean in the wrong direction and slows down the walk progress. The first turtle over the finish line wins.

RELATED ACTIVITIES:

Any type of family style games and entertainment.

MATERIALS:

Turtles, turtle race rig, field marker, whistle ribbons, festival flags, P.A. system, prizes, traffic cones.

POSSIBLE RESOURCES:

Turtle races come from people who are attending your total Special Event at the park or beach. Children, 8 and up, as well as adults enjoy playing this game.

CREATIVE PROMOTIONS:

This type of an activity can be promoted by land: "Turtles on the Run" at your local park or by shore (beach): "Sea Turtle Races" on the beach.

JUDGING CATEGORIES:

Place 1st, 2nd, 3rd over the finish line.

Judy Wilder, Department of Parks and Recreation, 4700 Recreation Drive, Virginia Beach, VA 23456-1449

TREASURE HUNT

DESCRIPTION:

Yo ho ho and treasure chest full of gold coins. This belongs to the first person who locates the buried treasure. All registrants (hereinafter known as pirates) receive their first clues in the mail. The clue directs them to a meeting place all pirates, at an appointed time, will gather for the second clue. The hunt begins at 9:00 a.m. and terminates at 9:00 p.m. with a gala pirates party. The final clue requires calculation as to the exact spot to dig reduce the likelihood of multiple winners.

RELATED ACTIVITIES:

Participants are encouraged to dress in costume for digging. All pirates wearing an eye patch are given a bonus by having one step marked off their treasure map.

RESOURCES:

Area businesses to form teams; different media to form teams. For youth participation contact schools, church groups, fraternities, sororities.

CREATIVE PROMOTIONS:

Send out press releases and public service announcements with "gold" coins.

The Learning Connection, Providince, RI; Course Trends.

SCARECROW ROW

DESCRIPTION:

Let Scarecrows invade your park setting or community and schedule events the entire family will enjoy. Begin with "Create A Scarecrow" workshop, where, for a small fee, all supplies are provided. The creations are then eligible for Scarecrow Row, where they are displayed and voted on by the public in one judging, and by a panel of judges in another judging. Spectators vote for their favorite three scarecrows.

ACTIVITIES:

"Become A Scarecrow:" enter the scarecrow races and win a prize for being the fastest to don a scare crow costume; "Pose with a Scarecrow:" hire a photographer to take photos of children and families with their favorite scarecrow; "Munch a Scarecrow:" include chocolate or gingerbread scarecrows in the concessions; "Buy a Scarecrow:" arts and crafts booths should include husk scarecrows dolls and door decorations; Mini-scarecrow contest: special 7" minature scarecrow competition; Scarecrow Stage: where entertainment occurs; square dancing, horse and wagon rides, pony rides, scary story-telling, scarecrow guitarist, street entertainers, river cruises.

MATERIALS:

Hay or straw, corn shucks, stage, judging and score sheets, prizes.

RESOURCES:

Businesses like to compete and challenge each other. Local stables, farmers market.

CREATIVE PROMOTIONS:

To advertise the scarecrow workshop, produce a teaser flier that shows the basic steps to creating a scarecrow.

JUDGING CATEGORIES:

Open Category - Open to groups, individuals, and families of any age, clubs and organizations. Chronicle Category for Business - must be sub mited and created by a "for-profit" business. Most creative category - all scarecrows are automatically entered in this category, which will be judged by a panel for artistic creativity. Public judging where the public votes on their 3 favorite scarecrows.

St. Charles Scarecrow Festival, St. Charles Convention and Visitors Bureau, P.O. Box 11, St Charles, 60174.

FAMILY MADRI GRAS STREET DANCE

Dress up the whole family for a night of fun and dancing in the street. The disc jockey or band plays music to please everyones tastes. Stage a costume parade and/or dance contest, as a part of the eve nings festivities. Invite area restraurants to sell samples from their menus.

BARK IN THE PARK

DESCRIPTION:

Here's a dog day afternoon that everyone can enjoy---even when dogs have been banned from your park(s). Who is the best behaved dog around? Or who is the tallest? And besides that, who has the most unusual name? All these questions and more, will be answered at "Bark in the Park." A significant element of the event is fund raising for the local humane society or Concerned Citizens for Animals, etc. Owners collect pledges prior to the event, promising contributors that the dog(s) and owner will participate in the 1K - K9 walk -- a short course marked off in the park. Awards are given to the three owners who have collected the most donations. All canine entrants receive a bandana to wear around their neck.

RELATED ACTIVITIES:

Contact pet stores, dog obedience schools, kennels, veternarians, dog food companies, to set up booths. Offer flea dippings, vacinations, and dewormings. Contests include Fetch and Catch contest, name contest, "Stupid dog tricks," Spuds McKenzie Look Alike contest, dog singing, beauty contest, photo contest. Have designated area for "bathroom breaks" for the dogs.

MATERIALS:

Pans of water, frisbees, animal food treats, prizes donated from pet stores.

POSSIBLE RESOURCES:

Humane Society, civic organizations, and pet stores. For participation: put fliers up in Veterinarian's offices.

CREATIVE PROMOTIONS:

Can tie in with October "National Adopt a Dog Month". A few weeks prior to the event, have staff members "walk invisible dogs" through your parks using the leash and collar gimmick. Build a large dog house and set up at another festival and hand out literature on the upcoming event. Make public service announcements using dog's "voice." Use a dog paw in visual marketing, such as fliers. Precautions: Specify that all dogs must be on a leash throughout the entire event and that any dog in heat is not permitted at the event. Request that all dogs competing be licensed and show proof of rabies vaccine.

JUDGING CATEGORIES:

Name contest: most unusual name, most appropriate name. Beauty Contest: longest hair, shortest hair, most unusual cut, tallest, shortest, friendliest, curliest, looks most like owner. Photo contest: Owners bring photos which are judged on best black and white, best color, best action shot, cutest, most unusual. Other contest: longest tail, shortest tail, best trick, best behaved.

City of Greenville Parks and Recreation Departments, 103 Cleveland Park Drive, Greenville, SC 29601

City of Charlotte Parks and Recreation Departments, 600 East Fourth Street, Charlotte, NC 28202-2864

AHH--
OUTDOORS....

NATURE

HANDS-ON PHOTO FIELD HIKE

Here's an event designed for all the nature loving photographers. Solict the help of a nature photographer who will take a group exploring through the woods. The photographer demonstrates techniques in the field using different types of equipment and lenses. Participants should bring camera, tripod, lenses, film, filters, outdoor attire and imagination.

RAINBOW HIKE

Find as many colors in nature, as possible, especially after a rain. This can be used as a contest.

PROGRESSIVE SUPPER HIKE

This is a three stop hike with different food and recreation at each stop, possibly ending with a campfire where songs, stunts and snacks bring the journey to a close.

STORY HIKES

Use a story (Alice in Wonderland, Treasure Island, etc.) to illustrate the hike. Lay the trail using phrasing and places from the story. The groups should be familiar with the story.

MAP HIKE

Each group is given a map which shows a route to take. This provides an opportunity to learn how to use a map.

NATURE ALPHABET

Divide into five groups. Give group 1 the first five letters of the alphabet and group 2, the next five, etc. Each group is to go out and find something in nature that will represent each letter, then bring it back. Upon return the entire group arranges the nature alphabet.

SQUARE YARD HIKE

Mark off a square yard on the ground and have campers find out how many different items they can find within it.

MONOGRAM HIKE

Find three or more nature objects beginning with your initials. If possible, collect the objects.

INCHER HIKE

Collect as many objects as possible that are one inch high, wide, around, long, etc. Objects can be measured, upon returning to see who brought the most. This helps kids notice the little interesting things that are usually overlooked.

SQUIRREL IN THE TREES

For ages 5-7. Couples join both hands to form trees. Within each tree stands a third child called a squirrel. The group stands in a circle formation. The leader selects an "It" who stands in the center of the circle and starts the game by calling out "Change." All of the squirrels in each tree must then change trees and "It" also tries to claim a tree for himself. The squirrel left without a tree goes to the center as "It", and the game starts again.

NATURE HIKE

A true nature hike encourages the observation of birds, insects, land animals, rocks, minerals, trees, shrubs, water animals and wild plants.

ADVENTURE HIKE

This is a journey leading to many points of interest, the discovery of unusual things in the nooks and byways of the trail. The group may be divided, each taking a different route in the search of adventure. All may return to a campsite and report their findings around the campfire.

WINTER WONDERS

For ages 5 to 7. How is snow made? What do plants and animals do in the winter? Explore these questions with participants. Include a hike; make a snow catcher and look at a snowflake under a microscope.

Chicago Botantical Garden, Glencol, IL - Course Trends

MYSTERY HIKE

Leaders carefully chart two or three different routes from point of departure to the goal of the hike. Directions are carefully hidden at several points, which tell, in turn, where the next directions are to be found. The crowd is divided into two or three groups and given directions where to find the next set of directions. The groups all finally arrive, by different routes at the same place, where fire, food and fun are provided.

BREAKFAST HIKE

Morning is the best time to observe the wildlife. Bring your binoculars, camera, and a breakfast snack sack.

GARDENING FOR WILDLIFE

Many native and cultivated plants serve as food and shelter for wildlife. Participants can learn how to attract colorful songbirds, butterflies and other animals to their yard.

NATURE SACK

Bird nests, leaves, fruit, etc. are placed into a paper sack. Players close their eyes and each handles all articles inside the bag. Blindfolds are removed. The winner is the one who records the largest correct number of articles.

MATCH YOUR HATCH

© Wilco

DESCRIPTION:

A series of fly fishing clinics, from viewing videos to discovering the local hot spots to fish will appeal to many ages. Schedule clinics for specific age groups and demographics to include teens', housewives, professionals, and senior citizens. Clinic topics could include selection and purchasing of equipment, tying the fly, matching the hatch, techniques of casting and reading the water (depths, and currents), rules and regulations, and locations to fish. The final clinic is a fishing expedition followed by a fish fry and awards ceremony.

RELATED ACTIVITIES:

Field trips to hunting and fishing retail store, or a factory which manufactures equipment.

MATERIALS:

Televsion, videos, fly fishing equipment and clothing, rods or make-shift rods from broom handles and string.

POSSIBLE RESOURCES:

State Fish and Wildlife Departments, Trout Unlimited for instructors, local hunting and fishing stores.

JUDGING CATEGORIES:

Fly Contest to include smallest, most authentic, most detailed, most unusual; first fish caught, largest fish caught, smallest fish caught, best fishermans hat, best dressed fisherman, most unusual dressed fisherman.

City of Greenville Parks and Recreation Departments, 103 Cleveland Park Drive, Greenville, SC 29601

INCREDIBLE EDIBLES

"If I knew you were coming, I'd have baked a catail root!" Wantto taste something wild? Then come and see what's cooking in the swamp! Learn about what plants are edible and how to prepare them.

ONE FOOT SQUARE

Divide the group into teams of fours. Place a book or other object over a piece of ground approximately one foot square. Give each group five minutes or less to collect as many living things as possible in that square. Reward the winning group with the opportunity to select the next earth-square.

RETRIEVING

Group is divided into teams of equal numbers of players. The leader holds up one specimen (rock, maple leaf, etc.) and says "Go!" Players are to find an item similar to that shown by the leader and one point is awarded to the group that first returns with a matching specimen. Play for ten or fewer points.

STOP, LOOK AND LISTEN HIKE

Hike for five minutes or a designated number of steps. Stop for one minute and write down all the objects you see or all the sounds you hear.

TWILIGHT BOAT FLOAT

Observe the diversity of aquatic life during one of the most fascinating times of the day - twilight.

BIG DADDY FISHING TOURNAMENT

Teams consist of one adult and one child, with trophies being awarded to the junior member of the winning teams. The event ends with a cookout.

MOUNTAIN STREAM ECOLOGY

Participants hike along the river investigating the plants and animals that make up the undisturbed mountain stream. Trout, aquatic insects, and mountain geology are among the subjects covered.

USEFUL MOUNTAIN PLANTS

Participants hike through the park or woods looking for plants that have been important to man from Indian times to present.

CREATURES OF THE NIGHT

When night falls a strange and often alien world comes alive. Bats and owls take to the night-sky, while toads and opossums prowl the surface. As Halloween draws near, offer "Creatures of the Night" to teach how these nocturnal animals carry out their lives in a world of darkness.

OWL PROWL

A night hike where participants search for owls, one of ntaure's most efficient hunters.

WOMEN'S FISHING COMPETITION

A three day fishing event geared toward female anglers.

NATURAL DYEING WORKSHOP

The pioneers used nuts, berries and other natural materials to produce dyes for their cloth and yarn. Participants learn what natural materials can be used for dyes and then have a chance to dye some yarn using these dyes.

WINTER TREE IDENTIFICATION

After autumn breezes have whisked the leaves from the trees, do they lose their identity until next spring? Participants step into the winter woods for an opportunity to identify trees through their bark, branches, buds and silhouettes.

CURIOSITY HIKE

Find some odd or curious looking objetcs such as bark, stone, stick, etc. Use imagination to tell what animal, etc., the object represents.

FAMILY CAMPOUT

Families bring their tents and campers for a weekend of family fun at your park. They enjoy three days of campfire programs, walks, an owl prowl and nature crafts.

EDIBLE AND MEDICINAL PLANTS

Observe the wide variety of wildflowers and discuss their medicinal uses. Different edible wild plants and their uses are also included.

FERNS AND FIDDLEHEADS

Ferns are one of the oldest plants on earth. At one time they were as large as trees, and dominated the world of the dinosaur. Participants learn about these fascinating plants and their life cycle. Program includes a hike to explore ferns in the area.

EVENING NATURE SHOW

Present a series of nature films, one every other week. Utilize films from the National Wildlife Federation such as "America's Wetlands," "Wildlife Refuges," "The Great Swamp," "The Sportsman," and "Ducks on the Wing."

ADOPT A TREE

Encourage participants to get to know their favorite tree a little better than just knowing its name. They will learn its height, width, age and how nature uses it as a resource. Participants receive an adoption certificate of the tree of their choice in their name.

TREE TAPPING

Participants will experience a little of the old world and excite their taste buds as they learn what trees to tap and how to turn their sap into sweep syrup.

FISHING ON THE ISLAND

This is a learning experience for ages 6-14. Require pre-registration and provide fishing equipment.

SHIPCRAFTER CLUB

Six to ten year old owners of radio controlled boats get together on the lake to operate their boats.

NATURE WALK SERIES

Utilize your various parks and schedule a series of hikes.

WINTER WONDERS

For ages 5-7. How is snow made? What do plants and animals do in the winter? Explore these questions with participants. Include a hike; make a snow catcher and look at a snowflake under a microscope.

Chicago Botanical Garden, Glencoe, IL, "Course Trends"

OUTDOOR FACILITATOR

Offer your center as a meeting place for outdoor-type clubs such as the Nature Plant Society, Walking/ Volksmarch Club, Sierra Club, Photography Club, Audubon Club.

CONSERVATION FAIR

Invite conservation and outdoor groups to your park in order to inform the public of their purpose and the activities they offer.

NATURE ERRORS

Prepare and tell a story containing errors. Points are scored for recognizing the errors. (Example: We were walking through a grove of Eucalyptus trees and stopped to fill our pockets with acorns which had fallen.) (Acorns are seeds of Oak trees.)

NATURE ALPHABET

First child in the circle names a bird, animal, or whatever is being played, starting with the letter A. Next child does the same with "B". Play on elimination or point basis.

SCAVENGER HUNT

Players are divided into teams. Each team is given a list of articles which are to be found and brought back to the playground within a certain time limit. The team first back with all of the articles, or the team having the largest number of articles at the end of time, wins the hunt. The articles should be things of little or no value which the children can get without disturbing the environment or City property.

1) Something Ugly
2) Something Beautiful
3) Something Funny
4) Something Sad
5) Hat
6) Feather
7) Six Different Leaves
8) Butterfly, Bugs
9) Pine Cone
10) Something Soft
11) Something Green
12) Something Brown
13) Something Fuzzy

14) Something Rough
15) Something Smooth
16) Large Rock
17) Medium Size Rock
18) Small Rock
19) Something Colorful
20) Something Hard
21) Lady Bug
22) Four Leaf Clover
23) Twig
24) Acorn
25) Wild Flower
26) Ant

SOCKS
AND
JOCKS....

ATHLETICS

INSTRUCTIONAL SPORTS CAMP/BEGINNER ATHLETE SPORT INSTRUCTION CLINICS (BASIC)

DESCRIPTION:

This is a one-day athletic program for beginner athletes, which integrates educational and recreational values by providing expert instruction and free-spirited play. The program is designed to introduce children to new sports and improve their skills in familiar ones. Children choose six sports and follow a rotating schedule, moving to different locations for each 50 minute clinic on a whirlwind sports "tour." Each participant is awarded a medal at the end of the day. Each instructor also chooses a "most promising" child in his sport based on attitude, sportmanship, effort and ability. These children receive an additional trophy award.

RELATED ACTIVITIES:

Lunch is provided for all participants and instructors. Bingo, with prizes, during lunch period is an enjoyable addition to the day's activities and allows the children to digest their food before the afternoon session. A movie could also be shown during this time.

MATERIALS:

Sports equipment, name tags, program schedules for participants and instructors, lunch supplies, "most promising" ballots for instructors.

POSSIBLE RESOURCES:

School teachers, coaches, parents, recreation instructors and personnel, local sport club members.

CREATIVE PROMOTIONS:

Program can be promoted to children as an opportunity to partici-pate in six different sport and earn a medal. Club organizations keying on the sport which interests the group.

JUDGING CATEGORIES:

"Most Promising" awards should be based on Attitude, Effort, Sportsmanship, Natural Talent and Physical Ability.

Melissa Bronez, Virginia Beach Department of Recreation, 800 Monmouth Lane, Virginia Beach, VA 23464

100 MILE CLUB

A great way of promoting fitness in your community have participants keep track of their mileage in a log book during a designated time period. Ride a bike 100 miles in 1 month, walk or jog 100 miles in 2 months, swim 100 miles in 3 months. Present awards at an annual program for those who acheive their goals. Award special citations (oldest, youngest, most miles in a year).

JUNIOR GOLF TOURNAMENT

Plan a golf tournament for the younger golfers in the area.

BIKE RIDE ACROSS YOUR STATE

DESCRIPTION:

Intermediate to experienced cyclists from age 18 - up can enjoy a six day recreational ride across their state with fellow bike enthusiasts. The Tennessee State Parks Departments maps out the route which takes participants to state parks where they tent camp each night. A sag service (vans) assists cyclists when they are too tired, ill or need help repairing their bicycle. One van leaves with early departures; one van leaves mid-way and one van waits until the last cyclist departs. Baggage trucks carry the tents, food clothing, musical instruments, etc. A $30.00 fee includes a t-shirt, camping and shower fee and a course map with a description of each state park where they will be camping.

ACTIVITIES:

Each night participants are entertained by an event at the park or by an area musician.

MATERIALS:

Banners at start and finish. Posters sent to towns and parks where tour will ride through. Rules and regulations sheet (must wear helmet, etc.) Recommended gear: tent, sleeping bag and pad, flashlight, sunscreen, towels, soap, toiletries, clothesline and pins, personal first aid kit, swimsuit, raingear, insect repellent, handlebar or seat bag, bike lock, helmet (mandatory), water bottles, cycling gloves, extra tubes, air pump, tire irons, patch kits, rearview mirror. Cyclists are responsible for their own transportation to origin of ride and upon completion of ride. An additional fee can be charged at pre-registration for bus transportation for person and bike back to origin.

RESOURCES:

Bike Federation or state or local biking club for sag service, state parks departments, musicians. For participation: bike clubs, Sierra Club, Outing organizations.

CREATIVE PROMOTIONS:

Advertise in State Park leisure guide, bike club newsletters.

Dare Bible, Tennesse State Parks, 701 Broadway, Nashville, TN 37203

TENNIS FESTIVAL

Week long series of tennis workshops clinics, and matches for every level of player.

BASKETBALL TURKEY SHOOT

Come and try your luck at shooting baskets and maybe win a turkey to take home for Thanksgiving. Participants accumulate points by competing in a variety of basketball activities (free throw, "21," H.O.R.S.E, Around the World). Grand prize winners get a turkey (donated by area grocery stores). Get participants from recreation centers, schools and basketball teams.

Kathy Fitz Gerald, Virginia Beach Recreation Center Bow Creek, 3427 Club House Road, Virginia Beach, VA 23462

ROUND BALL EXPRESS (BASKETBALL SHOWTEAM)

DESCRIPTION:

Hattisburg Recreation Department in Mississippi has created a sports program for 4 to 12 year olds that prepares them for high school basketball. The Round Ball Express begins with tryouts and ends with half-time performances at local high schools and colleges. There is diligent practice on the routine for three months (October thru December). Practice includes 3 hours at home each week working on tricks and skills. Team members are required to attend practice and to follow rules set out in the beginning. The Roundball Express (9 to 12 year olds) and the Coca-Cola Kids (4 to 8 year olds). The Roundball Express entertains the crowd with a routine of layups, passing, dribbling, shooting, rebounding, split posts, and slam dunk, while the Coca-Cola Kids perform their skills within a skit (all within 10 minutes). The back-ground music is that which Coco-Cola uses in producing their current commercials. All uniforms are red and white and the basketballs are red, white and blue.

ACTIVITIES:

Show the team videos of famous basketball players and games. Schedule basketball games between the team. Plan a party and/or field trip(s) to give the team a break from practice. Have ball girls on the side lines to retrieve the balls in order to keep the routines moving smoothly.

MATERIALS:

Promotional music from Coca-Cola, uniforms, sweat pants and shirts, hollowed-out Coke Machine from which Coca-Cola kids pop out when beginning their skit.

RESOURCES:

Converse Shoe Company: travel bags, practice shirts, shoes greatly discounted, contacts for "big games"; Coca-Cola Bottling Company: uniforms, refreshments, portable goals (7 1/2 feet), truck to transport equipment, sound equipment, two coaches; Radio Station: promotional spots, cuts tapes for routines, D.J. for show. Participants: from basketball and baseball leagues.

PROMOTIONS:

TV talk show appearances, school newspapers, radio stations that appeal to the youth.

JUDGING CATERGORIES:

Judges are not the coaches who are coaching the team, but area high school or college coaches and players. Tryouts are in a large arena so players can be judged on what they can do in front of a crowd. They are judged on behavior, ability to take directions, skills and tricks. Tryouts include a "showout" or "show off" time.

Mike Smith, Hattiesburg Parks and Recreation Department, 1812 Hardy Street, Hattiesburg MS 39401

CHILI SOFTBALL TOURNAMENT

Here's one way of getting the public to attend your softball tournament. During the cooler part of the season have a chili cookoff in conjunction with a major tournament and after judging, charge for the bowls of chili.

VOLKSMARCH

DESCRIPTION:

A volksmarch is an organized walk which covers a distance of 10 or 20 kilometers (approximately 6 or 12 miles). It is a leisurely walk through scenic or historic areas and is designed to appeal to everyone; all ages and stages of physical fitness. It is not a contest of speed or endurance; participants travel at their own pace (walk, jog, run), but must complete the event before finish time. Adequate time (at least four hours) is available to complete the event. One of the bonuses of volksmarching is that each participant who purchases a start card and completes the course receives an attractive souvenir, frequently a medal. Start cards are stamped at each checkpoint and verified at the finish line, where the participant will receive his medal. After establishing a route, the responsibility following include drawing a map, producing and distributing registration forms, deciding on an award and staffing the checkpoints.

RELATED ACTIVITIES:

Schedule a volksmarch as a single event or in conjuction with another activity, such as an arts or cultural festival or within Oktoberfest festivals. A volksmarch could be a fund raiser for a cause such as The Statue of Liberty. The European countries provide beer and bratwurst stands upon the finish of their marches.

MATERIALS:

Maps, check point sheets, pencils, registration forms, directional signs, water, cups, tables, chairs, tent (optional), awards.

POSSIBLE RESOURCES:

Since volksmarching is becoming increasingly popular, many recreation departments are programming sanctioned volksmarchs, which are instrumental in bringing in tourists to the area. Sanctioned volksmarches can be revenue producers. For information write: American Volkssport Association, Suite 203 Phoenix Square, 1001 Pat Booker Road, University City, Texas 78148

CREATIVE PROMOTIONS:

Use a German flair in the advertising. A radio spot where the German teacher is introducing the word "volksmarch" would get attention, as would an om pah band.

JUDGING CATEGORIES:

Awards are presented to everyone who registers for one and who completes the walk. Awards can be medals, ceramic plates, walking sticks, etc. Patches could also be on sale.

City of Greenville Parks and Recreation Departments, 103 Cleveland Park Drive, Greenville, SC 29601

FITNESS CHALLENGE

Choose your contender and prepare for the Fitness Challenge! Seven to eleven years olds, especially, like to challenge another individual. Child vs. child, parent vs. child or child vs. teacher/recreation leader are timed to see how many sit ups, how many push ups and how many jumps over the jump rope they can accomplish within a certain period of time. The best 2 out of 3 wins, and the challenge is repeated through out the year. To kick off the Fitness Challenge, arrange to have a presenter come in to speak on the importance of fitness and nutrition.

Ann Witwer, Todd Elementary, Spartanburg, SC

OKTOBERFEST SPORTS CLASSIC

DESCRIPTION:

Do as the Germans do, and bring in fall in a festive mode. Plan a 2 - 3 day event with a series of athletic events and exhibitions and offer German food and beverage under a big tent. Assign an event coordinator to each sport: road race, fitness walk, race walk, bike race, tournaments or exhibitions in tennis, softball, badminton, racquetball, handball, grass volleyball, youth league football, flag football, indoor or outdoor soccer, wheelchair basketball, wheelchair tennis, basketball shootout, swim meet and, of course a Volksmarch (See page 74).

RELATED ACTIVITIES:

Add to the festive flair by having an a German ompah band and dancers. Work with a local German-American organization to coordinate a German dinner the evening preceeding the sporting events. Volkswagon Beauty Contest (See page 56).

MATERIALS:

Registration forms, pencils, starting pistol, water cups, tables, chairs, directional signs on routes and on site, awards, PA system, maps, tents, cash, cash box.

POSSIBLE RESOURCES:

For Assistance: Secure the co-sponsorship of a local sporting goods store for the primary sponsor, who can provide t-shirts, advertising and obtain manufacturers for sponsorships of each event. For example, Saucony is approached to be the sponsor for the Road Race; Dunlop is approached to be the sponsor of the Tennis Tournament. In return for your department advertising the manufacturer as the event sponsor -- "Saucony presents the Oktoberfest Sports Classic Roadrace" -- on the event registration form, include their logo's on the poster and any display ad placed in the newspaper offer sponsors the opportunity to display and/or sell their merchandise at the event. The event sponsor will be asked to provide their product as prizes.

Have an executive committee comprised of 4 - 5 organizers (Athletic Director, Spercial Events Director, Marketing Director for sporting goods store). Organizers are responsible for finding sponsorships, market ing, planning events to be held, dates, times and selecting of event coordinatoors. Event coordinatoors are responsible for projected budget, projected participation, suggested prizes, marketing possiblilites. assistance is also criticial from local sports organizations, such as, track club, bike club, volleyball club, volksmarch club or Volkssport Association, sporting goods stores, bike shops, bicycle manufacturers, German-American club, german restaurants.

Food and beverage companies also appreciate the opportunity to give their product away and/or offer coupons at the event. Invite vendors for yogurt, bottled water, soft drink, sports drink, in addition to the Geman food.

CREATIVE PROMOTIONS:

Use German dialect in radio spots. Schedule volkswagon beauty contest a few weeks prior to event and plan to have the winning entries displayed at the Oktoberfest. A car dealer could display all entries and offer a free drawing for a car or trip.

JUDGING CATEGORIES:

Cash prizes in road race categories. T-shirts to first 10 teams to register in volleyball tournament and trophies to winning teams. Cash prizes to bike race winners and medals to volksmarchers.

City of Greenville Parks and Recreation Departments, 103 Cleveland Park Drive, Greenville, SC 29601

TURKEY CALLING CONTEST

DESCRIPTION:

This one day event can attract both amateur and professional callers who come dressed in their best hunting gear. After paying their entry fee the participants call in an order determined by a draw. The top ten in each catergory enters the finals. All participants are required to know all of the calls, with five calls being required in the competiton. Trophies are awarded to winners who are judged by professionals involved in conservation, hunting and outdoor activities and considered experts in their field. Admission is charged to the public.

RELATED ACTIVITIES:

Decorate the stage as an outdoor setting, to lend as much authenticity for the callers as possible. Invite exhibitors of outdoor and hunting gear and equipment to display and/or sell their merchandise and services. Include a junior division. Another activities could be a hunting dog show.

RESOURCES:

Wild Turkey Federation of the Southeast (club of turkey hunters and callers).

JUDGING CATEGORIES:

Amateurs are judged on the tree call of hen in spring, old hen yelp, cluck, and the person's own choice of their best call. Professionals are judged in the same categories, with the exception of the cluck, which is substituted for cutting of the hen. The winners of this competition are eligible to enter the World Champion ship.

Kay McCreery, Montgomery Parks and Recreation Department, 1010 Forest Avenue, Montgomery AL 36106.

FLASHLIGHT GOLF TOURNAMENT

Tired of losing your golf balls...no more; because they glow! So you say you don't play golf because you get home after dark...Perfect, because tee off time for the Flashlight Golf Tournament is at midnight--or anytime after dark. These are two great beginnings for advertising this "glow in the dark" event. Participants are responsible for their own clubs and flashlights (bulbs not to exceed a certain wattage). Use Scramble Golf (see page 78) rules. Each player is given a black t-shirt with a glow in the dark flashlight symbol on front and back. Every five to ten minutes a search light is shined on a 360 degree circle to recharge everyones shirt. Print posters advertising the event on black poster board using flouresant paint. Other flashlight events could be a frisbee golf tournament or glow in the dark rubber egg toss.

FITNESS FUN CONTEST

Children in different age groups participate in push-ups, sit-ups, standing long jump, jump ropes, basketball free throw, softball throw, limbo contest. Awards of certification and trophies are given.

ADVENTURE EXPO

DESCRIPTION:

Adventure Expo and various high adventure outings is challenging to both the participant and the recreation programmer. After selecting and planning the sports (advanced scuba, hang gliding, rapelling, cross country bicycling, whitewater rafting, skydiving), arrange to have an expo where representatives from each of the companies (hang gliding - Kitty Hawk Hang Gliding School) is on hand to answer questions about the sport.

RELATED ACTIVITIES:

Have simulators, videos, models, picture slides, brochures and equipment to show what the sports are all about. Offer discounts for early registration.

MATERIALS:

Booths and/or tables chairs, audio video equipment, brochures.

POSSIBLE RESOURCES:

Kitty Hawk Kites Hang Gliding School, Nags Head, NC; local or state bicycle club; whitewater rafting outpost; parachute center.

CREATIVE PROMOTIONS:

Produce a booklet to distribute before and during the Expo advertising the Expo and describing each sport, and other information (dates, time, fees, and necessary equipment and pre-requisites.)

Special Services, MCAS, Cherry Point, NC

FREE FOOT SCREENING CLINIC

With the cooperation of a podiatrist, conduct a screening for the detection of planter warts, athlete's foot and other foot diseases. The diagnosis is free, but no treatment is given. Have the clinic at a swimming pool or health club facility where showers are required or strongly encouraged. Ask your local podiatrist to help with your clinic, free of charge, with the potential of acquiring new customers. Include in the publicity the estimated value of the service provided at the clinic.

NO THANKS. I'D RATHER WALK!

For those who prefer walking as their activity, plan a day of events for every level of walker. Include a Volksmarch (see page 74), a shorter fitness walk, a race walk and a race walk clinic. The fitness walk is a 2 mile or 5 mile non-competitive walk. The race walk is a 6.2 mile walk, and if you choose, it can be sanctioned by The Athletic Congress (TAC), in your state. Have an experienced race walker(s) lead a clinic the evening or morning prior to the race walk to teach the techniques and rules of the sport. Some participants who want to practice their new race walking techniques on a shorter course may want to register for the fitness walk instead of the race walk.

SHORT STUFF BASKETBALL

Play a tournament using 9 foot goals and requiring all players to be under 6 feet tall.

RUN FOR FUN

A running event for kids ages 6 -12. Participants run each day for 30 school days and mileage is added up.

CANNONBALL

A combination of softball, baseball and slowpitch softball. Pitchers pitch overhand. Runners may lead off and steal. Batters can bunt and runners can be picked off. Game is played with an 11 inch softball.

SCRAMBLE GOLF

Scramble golf is a proven fun tournament played and enjoyed together by low handicap golfers and once-a-year golfers, alike. Scramble golf encourages a team atmosphere and speeds up normal play. Each foursome is a team. Each player in each group hits a tee shot on every hole. By group decision, the best drive is selected and left where it lies. Each of the other players picks up his/her ball and hits from the spot that was selected as the best. When all four have hit, the best shot is again selected, and again the other three balls are picked up and moved to the best spot. Again, the four players hit from the best spot. This process continues until a ball is hit into a cup. Although there is only one score per group, each person gets to hit every shot and be a part of the team's score. If there are not four players in a group, one player will play an extra ball. Prizes are awarded to the winning team and if individual scores are kept, prizes can be awarded to individuals with the best scores. Refreshments can be served as each group makes the nine hole turn. A banquet or barbecue could follow tournament play and provide an opportunity to present awards.

Illinois Parks and Recreation Association

TRACK AND FIELD CLUB

DESCRIPTION:

A track and field club formed to serve all age groups in amateur track and field sports can provide a three-fold purpose. 1) responsibilty for the production of drug-free and alcohol-free track and field events, 2) substance awareness education, and 3) track and field training for all ages that are members of the club. The club schedules four track meets annually. Divisions are: Bantam (10 & under), Midget (11 - 12), Youth (13 - 14), Intermediate (15 - 16), Young (17 - 18), Open (19 - 29), Masters (30 & over).

ACTIVITIES:

Elect a slate of officers and appoint chairmen to standing committees: Finance, Program, Membership, Training, Publicity. Prepare by-laws and guidelines for the organization. Include by-laws for membership, attendance, officers and committees (their duties and responsibilites), meetings, parliamentary procedures, order of business. Give the club a name. The City of St. Petersburg Florida calls their's "STRIDERS".

RESOURCES:

For assistance; coaches, media, schools, sporting goods stores. For participation; students, church groups, special interest groups.

CREATIVE PROMOTIONS:

Use area schools for distribution of membership applications. Provide a newsletter and send to members reminding them of meetings, fund raisers, and upcoming meets. Get the co-sponsorship of a radio station that gears itself to teens.

JUDGING CATEGORIES:

At each of the four meets, charge a fee which will cover a t-shirt and operating cost. Participants can enter up to five of the following events: 100, 200, 400, 800 meter, 1 mile run, 110 and 310 hurdles, 4 x 100 relay, long jump, triple jump, high jump, shot put, and javelin.

Bob Valenti, City of St. Petersburg, Leisure Service Department/Recreation Division, P.O. Box 2842, St Petersburg, Florida 33731

MARATHON SOFTBALL GAME

Kids, youth teams, church teams, civic clubs, etc. sign up to play for certain hours. A large scoreboard keeps count of innings. Marathon begins at 8:00 a.m. and ends at 10:00 p.m.

YOUTH TRIATHALON

Like a regular triathalon, the youth triathalon is comprised of three events - swimming, running and bicycling. The distances can be shorter, but the participants should have prior training. A helmet is required for the cycling event. Your department could plan seminars and training programs for 2 months prior to the triathalon.

Largo Recreation and Parks Department, P.O. Box 296, Largo, Florida 34649-0296

RAP (RECREATION AND POLICE)

DESCRIPTION:

RAP provides constructive, leisure time activities and the opportunity for teens to experience the positive influences from recreation specialists and the police department. Police and recreation personnel collaborate in all stages - planning, implementing, and execution of activities. The recreation department markets the event and the police assist in distributing free admission tickets, staffing and even coaching. RAP focuses on the 13-17 year olds and most activities occur when the school system is closed. Four events comprised the City of St. Petersburg, Florida's first RAP program. To fund the program, ask for the support of the Chamber of Commerce, who can release their membership list. Write local businesses for their monetary, in-kind services or prize donations. Four events/activites -- a basketball league, pool parties, an "Anything Goes" event, and a co-ed volleyball tournament -- comprised St. Petersburg's first RAP program.

BASKETBALL LEAGUE

Each site has 2 teams - the 13-15 year olds and the 16-17 year olds (no varsity players, 18 year olds, or graduates allowed). Each team is outfitted with a numbered basketball shirt in their team colors and has 2 coaches - one a police officer (one who is actually interested in basketball) and the other, a recreation leader. The league lasts 10 weeks and the teams practice one hour each week and have one game each week. A round robin tournament preceeds a two-night final four playoff at a high school or college gym. T-shirts are given as door prizes to encourage neighborhood children to attend.

POOL PARTIES

Pool parties are scheduled every Saturday night and admission is by ticket, only. Tickets are available from uniformed policemen. The event is restricted to 13-17 year olds. Free swimming games and contests are led by recreation personnel. Four policemen are in attendance - one is uniformed, but the other three are in shorts and swimsuits. Local disc jockeys donate their time and provide entertainment. DJs also advertise the event beforehand. T-shirts are given as door prizes. If your deparment has more than one pool, vary the locations of the pool parties from weekend to weekend.

ANYTHING GOES

This is a day or night of games held at a large park. Teams of 12 members are formed from recreation centers, church groups, YMCA's, YWCA's, and other youth organizations. Prizes are given in every event and trophies are given to the three top teams. The manpower for the event is a large pool of recreation personnel and police officers. After the games, a local disc jockey joins in with music, and the pool is open for a free swim. Each player receives a RAP t-shirt and sun visor.

CO-ED VOLLEYBALL TOURNAMENT

This is a one-day event. Letters are sent to church groups and youth organizations and teams are required to sign up in advance. Nine member teams play fifteen minute games in round robin fashion. Each participant receives a RAP t-shirt and sun visor. Police officers and recreation staff are the personnel. Tournament is followed by a pool party.

RELATED ACTIVITIES:

End the RAP program with a family picnic to include all participating police and their families. Have the sponsoring radio station provide a live remote. Set up games for spontaneous team play.

MATERIALS:

Admission tickets for uniformed police to distribute, detailed memorandums to police outlining entire program and ticket distribution.

RESOURCES:

Chamber of Commerce for area business listings, Police Department, Civic organizations, area businesses for personnel. For Participation: Youth organizations, churches, recreation centers, summer camps, schools.

CREATIVE PROMOTIONS:

Get a radio station behind this event and get their assistance in recording a clever public service announcement playing on the police involvement and/or the acronym, RAP.

City of St. Petersburg, Department of Leisure Services, 1450 16th Street North, St. Petersburg, FL 33704

BEAT FEET....

ROAD RACES

WOMEN'S ROAD RACE

DESCRIPTION:

Although female participation in co-ed road racing has increased, women find great satisifaction in an event programmed just for just them. A 1, 3, and 5 mile road race can be the encore to a series of running clinics, which have preceeded the race. Consecutive topics for the 10 week clinic series include: Getting started, safety, running shoes, pulse and stretching, racing techniques, nutrition and weight control. The clinics should be held near the upcoming race location. Immediately following the clinic and appropriate warm-ups, small groups, under the leadership of track club members, either walk or run the course.

RELATED ACTIVITIES:

Organized child care is provided during the clinics. A final seminar can be held the evening prior to the race. Nutritious beverages and snacks are provided, along with a local or national female athlete as the guest speaker.

MATERIALS:

Registration forms, safety handouts, pencils, films, fruit, water, cups, starting pistol, P. A. system, stage, tables, chairs, EMS, start/finish banners, finish chute, time clock, mile splits, awards, packet handouts.

POSSIBLE RESOURCES:

Local track club, corporations, sporting goods stores, Girl Scout troops (child-care).

CREATIVE PROMOTIONS:

Select a catchy name for the race, such as "Run Jane Run", (Liberty Life, Greenville SC), Women on the Run (Women on the Run, Inc. Greenville SC). Seek co-sponsorship with local television station and ask their anchor lady to do 30 second spots advertising the clinics and race. A section printed in the newspaper on Monday could be dedicated to the upcoming Wednesday clinic topic.

JUDGING CATEGORIES:

The extent of co-sponsorship has allowed some race coordinators to provide running outfits to every entrant, along with medals as the runner crosses the finish line. Cash prizes are awarded to the top ten finishers in the five mile race.

City of Greenville Parks and Recreation Departments, 103 Cleveland Park Drive, Greenville, SC 29601

FAMILY FUN RUN

Get the family out for a walk or run in the park. Design a course and everytime a family member walks or runs by the start point, they get a point. The event is timed and prizes are awarded at the end for the most points, largest family participating, oldest participant and youngest participant.

SHORT, FAT GUYS ROAD RACE

This may be a larger spectator event than participant event, because to qualify, the contestant's waist must be a least 4 1/2" larger than his inseam. A 3.1 mile race such as this is held in Skaneateles, NY. The event features beer, pizza, pretzels, Twinkies, and even smokes, along the course.

COSTUMED RUN AND CENTIPEDE RACE

For an added event at one of your scheduled road races include two other races-- a costumed run and a centipede race -- both run on a designated short course. These costumed runners and centipede racers are ineligible for awards in the regular (5,000 meter run) road race. Costumed runners are individuals wearing a costume of her/his choice. Centipede teams must consist of 6 runners and typically depict a theme, such as a 6 pack of beer, a side of a record album (each person is a song on an LP), six different fruits, etc. The costumed runners and centipede teams are judged on originality (Grand, 1st, 2nd, 3rd) and final time is not a factor in the judging of costumes.

OVERALL RULES:

1. All participants must exhibit a running number.

2. All recipients of awards must complete their course; time not a factor in judging costumes.

3. Each centipede must consist of 6 runners, no more and no less, to be eligible for awards.

4. Members of the centipede team must be joined together.

5. All centipedes and costumed runners must be at your park two hours before the race for judging.

6. Any protests must be registered with the Race Director prior to the awards ceremony.

Charlotte Parks and Recreation Departments, 1900 Park Drive, Charlotte, N.C. 28204

RUNNER'S POKER

Determine age divisions and set up a course with assigned stations. Each time a runner passes through a station, he is handed a playing card. The top five times in each age group plays a game of poker and wins prizes from local businesses, such as sporting goods, game and hobby stores and restaurants.

ZOO RUN RUN

A fun run that is held in your local zoo.

BYPASS THE BYPASS

A run that is set up around a newly constructed highway in your area. A run that encourages good health and preventative heart bypass surgery.

DEPOT DAYS DASH

A 1 mile fun run that begins/ends at your local train station/depot. Offer a drawing for an AmTrak round trip ticket.

LONG RUN

A run that is held in cooperation with your local hospital and acts as a fundraiser for your local lung association.

MARATHON TUNE-UP

A 10K run that is held several weeks prior to a major local marathon. The winners receive gift certificates for a free physical at the local hospital or for a free car tune-up.

MINI-MARATHON

A marathon that uses 1/3 of the distance that a regular marathon uses for the swim, bike, and run.

RACE FOR THE CURE

A run that is held as a fundraiser for a specific disease (i.e. cancer, leukemia, etc.)

RICE RUN

A run that is held for people who have been married within the last year.

SUPER SIZZLER

A run that is held in the hottest month of the year in your area.

SCHOLARSHIP RUN

A run with proceeds going toward local high school or college scholarships.

TWO STATE TWO-STEP

A run that is held in conjunction with a recreation department in a neighboring state. At the finish line have local two-step dance groups performing.

AUTUMN BREEZE

A fun run held in October during the peak color season.

AUTUMN BRIES

A run sponsored by a local cheese manufacturer. The winner gets several pounds and varieties of "brie" cheese.

GOBBLER HOBBLER

A run held just before Thanksgiving. The winner receives a coupon for a free turkey at a local grocery store.

HEART AND SOLE
A run sponsored by your local heart association and tennis shoe company/sporting goods store.

SUBURBAN STAMPEDE
A fun run, 5K, 10K run(s) that is held in a suburb of a large city.

RUN FOR YOUR LIFEGUARD
A run that is held as a fundraiser for your local swimming pool. Contact your local lifeguards to "lead the pack" at the starting line. Allow them a three minute lead.

SOME LIKE IT HOT
A run that is held in conjunction with a chili cook-off or chili eating contest.

TOWER TROT
A run that is held on the tallest building in your city. Participants run up the stairs to the top and then back down to the lobby.

RUN FOR THE ROSES
The winner of the race gets a years supply (one dozen per week/month) of roses. Sponsored by a local florist.

FIRECRACKER MILE
The race is started by shooting off a firecracker rather than firing a starting gun. The run may feature a fireworks show that evening.

WILDERNESS RUN
A run that is held in your local forest preserve or nature preserve/park.

GRANDMA'S MARATHON
A run for all grandmothers, regardless of age.

HAPPY-HOUR HUSTLE
A 5K run that begins at 5:30 p.m. and ends up at a local restaurant/lounge. Each participant receives a coupon for a free beverage at the restaurant.

FROSTBITE FLUE
A 5K run that is held in December or January. Sweatshirt, mittens, or wool hats are given to each participant, rather than a t-shirt.

SPRING AHEAD
A run that is held on the specific day in the spring when you move your clocks ahead one hour.

TWOSOME TROT
A run where couples enter as a team. Their times are combined at the end of the race. The couple/two person team with the lowest combined time wins.

CAREER MOVE
A run for all local businessmen and women.

HOSPITAL HUSTLE
A run sponsored by your local hospital or for all local hospital employees.

SHAMROCK SHUFFLE
A run held on St. Patrick's Day. Green t-shirts are a must!

TWILIGHT RUN
A run that begins at sunset.

RUN FOR THE HEALTH OF IT
A run that is held during National Physical Fitness Week/Month.

MINI-MILER
A 1 mile fun run for youngsters 8 years and younger.

SPLASH-PEDDLE-DASH TRIATHLON
A neat name for a triathlon that involves swimming, cycling, and running.

POLAR BEAR RUN
A run held in December or January.

K9-5K
A 5K run in which owners and their dog(s) compete as a team.

FOOTLOOSE FIVE
A 5K run that kicks off the summer season. Local radio station provides music throughout the race course.

HORTICULTURE HUSTLE
A run which is held as a fundraiser for the development of a local botanical garden.

MUSICAL MILE
A 1 mile run for all athletes that wear headsets and listen to music as they run. Local radio station/album store sponsorship is a must.

FRUSTRATING FIVE
A 5K run for all athletes who have never entered a 5K race before.

PANCAKE RACE
This race, which originated in Olney, England, takes place on the Tuesday before Ash Wednesday. Competitors must be women over 16 wearing traditional housewife's costume of apron and headcovering. With a toss and a flip of the pancake on the griddle, which one must carry, the ladies dash from marketplace to the parish church, where the winner receives a kiss from the ringer of the Pancake Bell.

RUN FOR THE PUMPKINS
A Halloween 5000 meter race. Participants run in pumpkins instead of t-shirts.

BEAUTY AND THE BEAST RUN
A relay event where one male and one female, each, run the same distance. Awards are based on combined times.

MIDNIGHT FUN RUN
This crazy event takes place on a golf course. Runners must pass by each hole. A party is held afterwards.

JINGLE BELL FUN RUN

A one or two mile run where participants can dress in Christmas attire or costumes. Every entrant receives bells to tie onto their laces. Prizes are awarded to the best individual and family costumes. (Comet the reindeer came as Comet cleanser). The entry fee is a five dollar toy which goes to underprivileged children.

RIVER TO RIVER RELAY

Teams of eight runners compete on a scenic 80-mile course.

IT'S YOUR LIFE. RUN IT.

Celebrate National Running and Fitness Day with foot and bicycle race, a senior stroll, and a fun run.

LUNACY RUN

Run under the light of the moon.

STAR TREK

Begins 15 minutes after sunset and is lighted by street lights and flashing barricades, and supervised by police.

RUN FOR THE REFUND

If a runner places in his/her division, their entry fee is returned.

RUN FOR THE BUDS

Co-sponsor this run with local nurseries and lawn and garden suppliers. Winners receive plants and garden supplies.

ONLY FOOLS RUN

A fun run on April Fools Day with lots of jokes played on the participants, such as total confusion at turns (arrows pointing in all possible directions, but every route leading to the finish line), the first water stop with no water in the cups (a second water stop with water is stationed nearby), and who else but the last person to come in is declared the winner?

LAKE VIEW RUN

A run around a large lake in your community.

Here are some great names for road races:

Cream of Wheaton	Run for the Animals
Gobbler Hobbler	Heaven Can Wait
Panther Pant	I Tried A Marathon
Run For Freedom	Santa Claus Run
Great Road Relay	September Stampede
Bridge To The Future	March Madness
Apple Blossom Bonanza	Fathers Day Frolic
Recovery Run	Masquerade Madness
Cranberry Crunch	September Sprint

'TIS THE
SEASON....

HOLIDAYS

BOO IN THE ZOO

DESCRIPTION:

This is an excellent alternative to the traditional trick or treating through a neighborhood. Civic organizations set up booths throughout the zoo. (They are charged a fee $50.00 - $100.00.) Candy is bought from one source and handled by recreation staff ONLY! A variety of candy should be bought; -- 1 cent a piece to 6 cents a piece. Bags are purchased and printed with sponsor's logo on front. Children pay ($2.00) to enter and receive a trick or treat bag, then walk through the zoo and collect candy at each station. Adults should be charged a minimum fee ($0.50) to enter. All staff and sponsors should dress in Halloween costume for the event. This event can be held for three nights, including Halloween night.

RELATED ACTIVITIES:

Have Casper's Friendly Castle (see page 88) set up in a separate building in the Zoo.

MATERIALS:

Each station (organization) is responsible for decorating their own table or booth. Materials provided would be tables, chairs, electricity, candy, trick or treat bags, money box and change.

POSSIBLE RESOURCES:

Police and fire departments, toy stores, VFW chapters, Junior League, pizza company, radio stations, any group or company that is youth-oriented.

CREATIVE PROMOTIONS:

Flyer sent to all day care centers in area, PSA's in newspaper, TV, and radio. Approach soft drink company for co-sponsorship; they give away product at event and help pay for bags and candy. Radio station should swap an agreed-upon amount of airtime to sponsors and the event in order to be a co-sponsor.

City of Greenville Parks and Recreation Departments, 103 Cleveland Park Drive, Greenville, SC 2960

GHOUL-A-GRAM

Spook friends with a Ghoul-A-Gram. The participants makes reservations with your department for Dracula, the Wicked Witch or other costumed characters to deliver a treat and balloon to a "spoocial" person. The cost is $5.00. You may want to limit the availiability of this service to the surrounding areas of your facility.

CASPER'S FRIENDLY CASTLE

DESCRIPTION:

Toddlers to mid-elementary school age children love Halloween, but at the same time many are terrified. Why not hold an event just for them -- a totally "unscary" event with favorites such as Casper the Friendly Ghost, "Count Dracula" from Sesame Street, live friendly scarecrows, the great Pumpkin, a fairy godmother and good witch? Or you can design rooms using local or national characters that are children's favorites (ex. ALF or a dinosaur room). Construct a friendly house divided into rooms where the characters greet them: scarecrows in the corn field; Casper, in a project room, where the children help complete a mural; "Count Dracula" assisting with the counting of Halloween items; and the Great Pumpkin, amoungest the smiling jack 'o' lanterns biding the children goodbye.

RELATED ACTIVITIES:

Outside the castle, set up kiddie carnival games and schedule a Halloween costume contest.

MATERIALS:

Costumes, hay, scarecrows, partitions, if necessary, art supplies, paint, props, pumpkins, candles, decorations, crepe paper streamers, balloons, lighting and sound.

POSSIBLE RESOURCES:

Deliver promotional flyer to day care centers and schools. Additional staffing can be provided by scout troops, university students, civic organizations.

CREATIVE PROMOTIONS:

Have Casper, ALF or the friendly scarecrow invite children to come visit their house on a 30 second radio spot.

City of Greenville Parks and Recreation Departments, 103 Cleveland Park Drive, Greenville, SC 29601

HALLOWEEN TAKE A TREAT

Have the children at your recreation center dress up in their Halloween costumes and deliver healthy treats -- apples and such -- to hospital patients, seniors or to retirement homes.

HALLOWEEN CAMP OUT WEEKEND

Select a special park with cabins, or pitch tents. Participants take a hayride to the "pumpkin patch" where they choose a pumpkin to bring back to decorate. Other events include a storyteller, nature walk, videos, costume contest, campfire and hot dog roast.

HALLOWEEN PARADE

On Halloween afternoon, have participants come to the recreation center in their costumes. Everyone marches to the neighborhood churches where the minister speaks on safety. Afterwards, in parade fashion, trick or treat throughout the neighborhood and then return to the center for a Halloween party.

HAUNTED FOREST

DESCRIPTION:

For a new twist at Halloween, convert one of your parks into a haunted forest. A dark wooded area, free of debris, can be an especially scary event for the three days prior to Halloween and Halloween night. The forest is made up of five to seven scare station's. A white life line leads the "victims" through the forest, stopping at the entrance of each station and starting again at the stations' exits. Victims are sent through in groups of four to six at a time. As a new group approaches a station, a ghoul scares them from behind into the station. It is important that the victims are scared from BEHIND in order to keep them moving along the trail. Ghouls should be dressed in dark clothes with faces painted in dark colors. The following committees are suggested: one for each scare station, publicity, lighting and sound, costume and make-up, concessions and parking, finance, and construction.

RELATED ACTVITIES:

Schedule a dress rehearsal two nights before opening night and invite the media, special population groups and prominent public figures.

MATERIALS:

Wood, chicken wire, cardboard, plastic, mattresses (to soften pathway in various places), paint, sheets. Props, to include: caskets, mannequins, mirrors. For special effects, use chainsaws, strobe lights, glow sticks, blowers, firecrackers.

RESOURCES:

For assistance: Get co-sponsorship of a civic organization, which can provide the personnel (Rotary, Jr. League). For preparation, contact all recreation centers.

CREATIVE PROMOTIONS:

Hang posters in the Haunted Forest (park) two to three weeks prior to Halloween, advertising the upcoming events. Record a scary radio public service announcement and/or get the co-sponsorship of a radio station that appeals to the youth.

Linda Hook, Georgia Southern University, Landrum Box 8073, Statesboro, GA 30460

LITTLE DEMON DANCE

A Halloween dance for children 6 to 12. Include a costume contest, dance contest, refreshments and disc jockey.

HALLOWEEN HUNT

Children are divided into two separate groups: pre-schoolers to 3rd graders on one side of the park and 4th to 6th graders on the other side. Before the event begins, candy is thrown on the ground, including six large slo-pak suckers. The suckers are marked with a number 1 to 3, and if found, children will receive a prize corresponding to that number. All age groups are lined up before the event begins for judging of costumes as well as instructions for the hunt.

TOYS FOR TOTS

DESCRIPTION:

To kick off the Christmas season, malls are always looking for innovative ways for Santa to arrive. Why not have Santa Claus lead a Toys for Tots Parade? In order to follow Santa in the parade, children must bring a toy to donate to needy children. After their procession through the mall, the children present their gifts to the U.S. Marines, who pile the presents on top of a Jeep stationed at the end of parade.

RELATED ACTIVITIES:

Encourage children to come dressed in colorful Christmas attire. Hold winter carnival games/rides inside or outside mall, depending on weather. Every parade participant receives a ticket coupon book in exchange for their toy donation.

MATERIALS:

Tickets for carnival.

RESOURCES:

U.S. Marine Corps; carnival vendor.

CREATIVE PROMOTIONS:

Mall signs, day care, kindergarden, elementary schools. Post signs at toy stores.

McAlister Square Mall, 225 S. Pleasantburg Drive, Greenville, SC 29605

CHRISTMAS BOAT ALONG

DESCRIPTION:

A unique way of Christmas Caroling is accomplished by having local boaters decorate their boats with Christmas lights, then parade through the waterways. The boats stop at various docks, landings and waterfront restaurants. Carolers could consist of a group of friends, Girl Scouts, Boy Scouts, civic organizations, choir groups, etc. Interested boaters meet with the recreation department 2 months in advance to appoint a lead boat, which is responsible for route, boat line up and pace.

ACTIVITIES:

The celebration begins with on-shore activities at a local park: turning on the park Christmas lights; boat arrival; band performance; intermission; boat departure; Santa arrives on a fire truck; choir entertainment and other entertainment.

CREATIVE PROMOTIONS:

Deliver flyers to homes on waterway asking for their participation. (Candles in windows and greeting boats as they appear.)

JUDGING CATEGORIES:

Have on shore spectactors judge boats for appearance: most colorful, most unique, most harmonious singers.

SANTA MOVIE

A free movie is sponsored by a local movie theatre on a Saturday afternoon in December while parents are Christmas shopping. Admission is a canned food item to be distributed later in Christmas baskets. Santa and Mrs. Claus are there to collect food and greet children.

WRAPPING BEE

DESCRIPTION:

A festive, communal wrapping session designed to give parents a chance to wrap without interference from kids, and with adequate space to work, and all combined with holiday spirit. The recreation department provides all materials, holiday music, adequate tables, chairs and refreshments. A flat fee should be charged for each participant ($5.00); or charge a certain amount per box wrapped.

ACTIVITIES:

Bow making workshop, wrapping contest, bag making workshop, paper decorating (homemade wrapping paper) workshop.

MATERIALS:

Wrapping paper, bows, scissors, tape, tags, tables, chairs, Christmas music and player, hot apple cider, Christmas cookies, candy canes, Christmas trees and stopwatch.

RESOURCES:

Junior League, florist, craftshop owner, and art teachers.

CREATIVE PROMOTIONS:

Senior citizens centers, malls - Santa Claus booth, craft shop, wherever bows are sold, pre-schools, newspaper.

JUDGING CATEGORIES:

Prettiest bow, most unique wrapping job of an unboxed item, specified package wrapped in shortest amount time.

SANTA BABYSITS

You're never too old to believe in Santa Claus and your center's Santa can make a believer out of moms who need to finish their Christmas Shopping -- alone. Santa greets the kids and shows them a movie, serves them lunch and spins the records at the afternoon dance. Include arts and crafts (gift making, wrapping paper making), games, Christmas cookie baking.

LUMINARIA

Encourage the participation of your community by sponsoring "Luminara" or "The Festival of Lights" on Christmas Eve. The Luminara are lighted candles in sand in paper bags lining both sides of the street and also driveways. The lights symbolize the bonfires the shepherds built to light their way to Bethlehem on the first Christmas Eve. Supplies needed : 1) paper bags (no. 5 or 6) to line street or driveway, spaced 8 or 10 feet apart. 2) sand to put about 2 inches in each bag. 3) Candle for each (about 6 inches). Prepare bag by turning down tops 2 inches, forming a cuff on outside. Space bags along street and driveway. At dusk on Christmas Eve, place candles in center of sand in bags and light. Candles should burn three or four hours. Luminara is most effective if decorative lights are turned off while candles are burning. The recreation department provides sand, only, and makes it available at a certain facility(s).

Jackson Recreation And Parks Department, Jackson TN

CHRISTMAS DOOR DECORATING CONTEST

When there's Christmas in the air, get your community into the spirit by holding a door decorating contest. Have the participant register their door around the 20th and present the award on the 23rd. Categories are: Most Original Door, Most Colorful Door, Nature's Greenery, Best Door, Best Old Fashion Christmas Door, Most Religious Door, Most Unusual Door, Best International Christmas Door, Best Children's Door, Best Science Fiction Christmas Door, Outstanding Family Door.

Morale Welfare Recreation, Charleston, SC

CHRISTMAS LONG AGO

A log cabin or a similiar atmosphere is a perfect setting for pre-schoolers up to second grade to enjoy holiday stories, songs, traditions and memories of the past, shared with the teacher (dressed in a colonial costume). The cabin can be decked out for the holiday with a Christmas tree, natural wreaths, garlands, fire in the fireplace, and the sweet smells of Christmas. Sugar cookies and warm apple cider are served. Offer this 25-30 minute presentation on a scheduled basis and require prior reservation.

BREAKFAST WITH SANTA

Make this an intergenerational event by asking your senior citizens to prepare breakfast for pre-schoolers. Reservations are necessary. Santa and Mrs. Claus will no doubt be two of your senior citizens who will listen to the wish lists and give out the traditional candy kiss.

ANGEL GIFT GIVING TREE

Share the Christmas Spirit by giving! Decorate a tree with paper angels. On each angel is written the name and age of a needy child. Commited people then remove an angel and purchase a gift for the child and bring to your center by a certain date. The gifts are either delivered or distributed by Santa at a party for the children.

LUNCH WITH SANTA

Plan this event during the week to make it exclusively a pre-school affair. Children bring their brown bag lunch to the recreation center and eat with Santa. Photos with Santa and Christmas carols follow.

CHRISTMAS AT THE COURTHOUSE

Deck the halls of your courthouse. Invite school groups to tour and get a chance to talk to the judge. Continue the festivities at night by inviting the public who is to be entertained by school chorus groups, bands, sign language groups and the courthouse employees community choir.

CHILDREN'S COTTONTAIL PARADE

DESCRIPTION:

Everyone loves a parade, and springtime shouts color, flowers, butterflies and birds. Mini-floats carrying costumed children, marching units, decorated bicycles, tri-cycles, wheelchairs, and both local and national characters, comprise a successful children's Easter parade. And who should lead the parade, but the Easter Bunny? A mini-float many times begins with a red wagon, as the wheels are already there. Float size should be limited to 5 feet by 7 feet and motorized vehicles excluded. A parade theme, such as "Springtime in the Mountains" varies the event each year and gives direction to the participants. Don't let the possibility of bad weather discourage you from holding an Easter parade; Main Streets are great, but so are malls.

RELATED ACTIVITIES:

Provide entertainment such as a puppet show or clown while judges tally scores. Schedule an Easter Egg hunt following the parade.

MATERIALS:

P.A. system, trophies, ribbons, judges sheets.

POSSIBLE RESOURCES:

Participants usually come from Girl Scout troops, Boy Scouts, Cub Dens, churches, neighborhood communities, PTA's, YMCA, YWCA, daycare centers and individual families.

CREATIVE PROMOTION:

At a local mall, schedule a mini-float and bonnet building workshop two or three weeks prior to the parade. Display a float and have frills such as ribbons, flowers, plastic bunnies and birds for the children to attach to an old hat they bring from home.

JUDGING CATEGORIES:

Best: wagon float, other float, unit, costume, Easter costume, bike, trike, stroller, wheelchair, all around, band, entry from a merchant, most original bonnet, finest Easter apparel, Easter theme.

City of Greenville Parks and Recreation Departments, 103 Cleveland Park Drive, Greenville, SC 29601

HOW TO BUILD A RED WAGON FLOAT

Converting a vehicle (wagon, stroller, tricycle) into a float is a simple thing. Use scrap wood, cardboard, paint and of course your imagination.

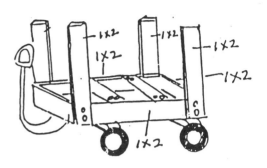

Using 1 x 2's build a tight fitting wooden frame around the sides of a little red wagon. Nail two 1 x 2's from side to side to support the frame. Nail 4 more 1 x 2's upright (for further support).

Glue and nail pieces of cardboard that you have cut out to size and shape to the wooden frame and erect 1 x 2's.

Paint and decorate the float. This was a chartreuse caboose in last year's parade.

Bonnets are great fun! Decorate an old hat with tissue or real flowers, bunny ears, carrots, buttons and bows, butterflies or any kind of Easter frills.

EGGSTRAVAGANZA

DESCRIPTION:

All of your recreation centers collaborate to present an Eastertime Eggstravaganza at one location. Each center is responsible for developing an Easter-themed game, such as a bowling game with pins shaped like rabbits, or a go hunting booth, and all prizes are some kind of a stuffed animal. Each center's art instructor is also responsible for bringing an idea and materials for a make-and-take craft.

RELATED ACTIVITIES:

Face painting, coloring contest, giant Easter mural, egg hunt, Easter videos, egg decorating contest, photos with the Easter bunny.

MATERIALS:

Games, prizes, relevant art supplies, plastic eggs, videos, Easter bunny outfit.

RESOURCES:

Appliance stores for large boxes for booths, promotional companies for prizes, video stores, costume supply company. For participants; pre-schools, scout troops, after school programs.

CREATIVE PROMOTIONS:

Invitations in the form of a coloring contest that can be entered in competition at the Eggstravaganza.

NOT THE SAME OLE EASTER EGG HUNT

To add "color" and "eggcitement" to your egg hunt and offer prizes to those who find one of these specially decorated eggs: Golden Egg (grand prize), Silver Egg, Striped Egg, Polka Dot Egg, Rainbow Egg, Glass Egg, Zig Zag Egg, Easter Lamb Egg, Peter Rabbit Egg, Biddy Egg, Jelly Bean Egg, Camouflage Egg.

Greensboro Parks and Recreation Department, Greensboro, NC

EGGCITEMENT AT THE ZOO

The Zoo celebrates Easter with a parade, bonnet contest, a magician, costume characters and, of course, real live animals! (see Cottontail Parade, page 93.)

FLASHLIGHT EASTER EGG HUNT

Older kids will find hunting eggs (or jellybeans) in the dark, fun and challenging. When the sun goes down the kids get out their flashlights and search for eggs. You won't have to hide the eggs behind things; the darkness is a big enough obstacle. Hide eggs in different areas of your park for different age groups.

PEACE POLE

Area churches unite at Eastertime to celebrate in both a religious and pagan manner. First, ministers are encouraged to present a special religious program at their church on Saturday morning. Afterwards, everyone from children to seniors gather at a large park for a cookout, entertainment and Easter Egg Hunt.

LEPRECHAUN LUNCHEON

DESCRIPTION:

Plan a day of fun and surprises with a Leprechaun Luncheon. Children arrive dressed in green, or perhaps like a leprechaun, and are entertained with games, music, refreshments and a treasure hunt. Older children can play a spelling game by seeing how many words they can spell using the letters from the word(s) Irish, lucky, rainbow, blarney stone. The younger children can search the building or playground for hidden paper sham rocks. The highlight of the day is the treasure hunt. Clues take the participants from one place   to another until they finally end up at the pot of gold. Here the Leprechaun hands everyone a bag of golden wrapped chocolate coins. (If the event takes place in a mall, participating stores will agree to give away a prize at each clue and the Leprechaun will be waiting at the last clue). Depending on the age group, children may need assistance with the map. Serve green food such as "Clover Punch," "Rainbow Sandwiches," (sand wiches made on green bread that the local bakery can bake), "Shamock Cookies" (cookies shaped like Shamrocks), green jello, celery, etc.

RELATED ACTIVITIES:

Take this opportunity to educate the participants on Ireland, the barney stone, and St. Patrick. Include Irish sing-a-longs, Irish jig instruction, and a costume contest.

MATERIALS:

Green and white paper products for decorations and invitations, prizes (small plants, herbs, favors from card stores, can of peas -- anything green), a "Leprechaun," refreshments, tables, chairs, PA system, stereo, records or tapes, treasure hunt.

POSSIBLE RESOURCES:

Notices to pre-schools and your mailing list for youth participants; library, card shops for ideas, decorations and prizes.

CREATIVE PROMOTIONS:

Invitations in the shape of a shamrock and/or a coloring contest, which also serves as a registration to attend the luncheon.

JUDGING CATEGORIES:

Person wearing the most green, person who resembles a leprechaun.

Nancy Callahan, Greenville Co. Recreation Commission, 500 Roper Mountain Road, Greenville, SC 29615

"LOVE IS..." PHOTOGRAPHY AND CALLIGRAPHY EXHIBITION AND SALE.

DESCRIPTION:

Valentine's Week is a most appropriate time for photographers and calligraphers to exhibit and sell expressions of love. Work in conjunction with a local mall or art gallery for display and/or prize money. Work with photography clubs and calligraphy clubs in establishing entry criteria. Advertising for the event should be at least three months prior through flyers (entry forms) and public service announcements.

MATERIALS:

Display panels, prize ribbons, prizes, judges.

CREATIVE PROMOTIONS:

Use the expression "pictures speak a thousand words" in the radio advertising.

JUDGING CATEGORIES:

Photography: Best: color, black and white, candid shot, group picture, over-all, and honorable mention. Calligraphy: Most original quotation, best executed expression, most artistic adaptation, over-all, and honorable mention.

VALENTINE VIDEO RAMA DANCE

Preteens and teens celebrate Valentine's Day with their sweethearts by dancing to favorite videos, competing in a famous rock star look-a-like contest and "Lip-Sync" contest. Special effects could include a D.J., spotlight and disco ball. You could plan ahead and have the kids make lip sync videos to play the night of the dance.

VALENTINE DESIGN CONTEST

Hold this event at a recreation center or plan it as a community-wide event to attract "professionals," as well. Entries could be displayed at the recreation center, mall, bank, or art gallery/museum. Designate age groups and categories and have participants use their own imagination and materials to create their masterpiece. Judging catergories: Most original, most elaborate, most unusual, most comical, most serious, most authentic (old fashioned), most charming, most ridiculous. (Have amateur and professional divisions.)

VALENTINE MAKING WORKSHOP

Offer several activites in order to include all age groups. Younger children make valentine cards while older participants make cloth heart (7") sachets for Mom using the sewing machine or hand stitching. Small leather are crafts most suitable for men. This can be held at a recreation center or in a mall.

"HEARTS DELIGHT DELIVERY SERVICE"

Offer a Valentine delivery service through your recreation center. "Cupid" will deliver a gift to sweethearts, along with a bouquet of balloons for $5.00, or the price you set. Gifts should be at the recreation center Febuary 13 for the next day delivery.

VAL-A-GRAMS VALENTINES

A unique way to say "I Love You" is by offering a service where your recreation center will send loving messages to sweethearts via telephone (local calls only). Provide a selection of poems, quotes or mes sages and the sender can choose one or write his/her own. State a deadline of four daysprior to Valentine's Day and charge $1.00 per message.

SHARE A VALENTINE

Schedule a valentine making workshop at your center and ask each participant to leave one valentine behind. On Valentine's Day, take your pre-schoolers, all dressed in red and white to nursing homes, retirement homes and your senior citizen center to deliver the valentines. Treat your pre-schoolers to an ice cream cone afterwards.

VALENTINE COOKIE AND/OR CANDY WORKSHOP

For adults or children, this event can provide gifts for loved ones, or might be extended into a money making event by selling the product to the public. Contract a candy making instructor, if your staff has no experience in candy making.

LIVE SINGING VALENTINES

The musically talented participants at your recreation complex can comprise a group(s) of traveling minstrels to deliver a special "package" to loved ones. The package consists of: 1 song from the heart; 1 delicious pastry; and 1 certificate of caring. Customers pay $3.00 per Valentine.

Sandpiper Recreation Center, Building 720, Ft. Story, VA

POST TURKEY DAY WORKOUT

Most fitness centers are closed the day after Thanksgiving, so why not open your doors to a two hour aerobic/exercise class for those conscientious exercise buffs who might have just over endulged on Turkey Day? This is a proven money-maker for your center.

Here are some other Holiday events that might spark some creativity:

NEW YEARS
Publication of communtiy residents'
    New Years resolutions
New Years Eve Party
New Years Baby Costume Contest
Polar Bear Swim
Community New Year's Day Parade
Decorated Diaper Contest

HALLOWEEN
Great Snoopy Pumpkin Hunt
Halloween Carnival
Great Pumpkin Beauty
Trick or Treat On Ice
Halloween Costume Dance
Spooks, Spares and Strikes

VALENTINES DAY
Cupid's Calling
Daddy-Daughter Dance
Valentine Card Contest
Cupids, Cookies & Cards Tournament

THANKSGIVING
Turkey Chase, Trot & Shoot
Outdoor Turkey Cookout
Turkey Wing Arm Wrestling

ST. PATRICKS DAY
Irish King & Queen Crowning
Shamrock Parade
Green Kite Flying Contest
Leprechaun Look-A-Like Contest
Irish Carnival

CHRISTMAS
Santa Visits Homes
Christmas Candy Contest
Christmas Decoration & Ornament Contest
Santas Treasure Hunt
Santa's Calling
Christmas Party On Ice
Country Christmas Bazaar
Christmas Crossword Puzzle
Santa's Mailbox
Santa Claus Look-A-Like Contest
Yule Log Hunt & Burning

EASTER
Easter Bonnet Contest
Visits with the Easter Bunny
Easter Rock Hunt
Easter Eggstravaganza
Easter Egg Contest

DO IF YOU DARE....

???

PARTY IN POOR TASTE

DESCRIPTION:

Have you ever wanted to throw a party for all your friends, but didn't want to go to all the work? If so, a Party in Poor Taste will get you off the hook! There's no need to clean up your house, run the dishwasher, or stock up on food and beverages for your guests, because that would be in good taste. Only things opposite from normal and polite are allowed. Invitations with vague directions and a somewhat confusing map should be sent out on greasy, brown paper lunch bags. When your guests finally arrive... don't be polite and greet them at the door; simply say "Come on in, the door is open." Then... the fun begins.

RELATED ACTIVITIES:

Have both the stereo and TV going at the same time and at the same volume level. Set out a deck of cards with only 49 cards in the deck: Make guests get their own food and drinks: Have spotted glasses for the guests to put their drinks in; if they want to wash their glass, they may, but they have to dry it with a "cruddy" dishtowel: Don't provide garbage containers for guests to put their empty beer cans in: Don't empty the ashtrays all night: Provide a roll of toilet paper that is just about finished, with no other "new rolls" to be found anywhere in the bathroom: Don't offer to make anyone's dinner: Leave hot dogs in their plastic packaging and have a plate of ground beef, but don't have any hamburger patties made up: don't provide any buns for the hamburgers or hot dogs; for the vegetarians, provide a loaf of white bread in it's plastic bag with the price tag still on, and a jar of peanut butter and jelly: Only provide one knife for both jars: Serve warm, generic beer and generic potato chips and chocolate chip cookies: When it starts to get late, tell your guest that you're tired and that they have to go home.

MATERIALS:

As little as possible!

POSSIBLE RESOURCES:

Your friends....if you have any!

CREATIVE PROMOTIONS:

Don't promote it. Simply send out the invitation and don't "follow-up" on them.

JUDGING CATEGORIES:

Best "poor taste" costume, best "poor taste" drink, best "poor taste" joke, best "poor taste" album or tape, best "poor taste" attitude.

City of Charlotte Parks and Recreation Departments, 600 East Fourth St, Charlotte, NC 28202-2864

MOTORIZED BAR STOOL RACE

Contestants build their own motorized bar stool. Specifications: 4 - 6" rubber wheels; powered by a 12 volt automobile starter motor; rear wheel drive and an 8" steering wheel; no brakes. The bar stools can go as fast as 30 miles an hour. The course is 750 feet long. Drivers must start in a sitting position and remain seated at all times. Pushing by the driver and cutting in are not permitted. After the race, contestants motor on down to the sponsoring bar and pull up to the bar.

SWIMMING FIN RACQUETBALL TOURNAMENT

Players must wear swimming fins while they play racquetball.

DOWN 'N' DIRTY DAY

Try this at summer camp. Include body painting, mud wrestling, tug of war (over a mud puddle), kick ball on a muddy field, slip-n-slide into a mud hole, and a fire department hose-down at the end of the festivities.

COW PLOP

DESCRIPTION:

This is a great fundraiser that can be run in conjunction with a large festival, or it can be "in a field all its own." A large field is divided into 400 two-foot squares which are then sold for $10.00 each. A snow fence makes up the four sides of the grid field. Each person purchasing a square receives a raffle ticket with a number on it. The second raffle ticket with that same number on it is then placed into a hat. Once all tickets have been sold, the raffle tickets in the hat are mixed up and then randomly drawn and placed on each of the squares. Cows enter the area, then everyone waits to see which square wins.

RELATED ACTIVITIES:

Include a "calf plop" held for youngsters and done on a smaller grid field. Prices for the raffle tickets are $1.00 instead of ten.

MATERIALS:

Snow fence or light weight construction site fencing, white paint to line the grid field on the grass, double raffle tickets, hat to mix raffle tickets in, cash box and change, PA system and music.

POSSIBLE RESOURCES:

Local dairy farmers.

JUDGING CATEGORIES:

The most "plop" on one square (selected from one of the three winning squares).

MUD DERBY

Have an annual competition where you allow the participants to "play dirty." Hold a mud derby and let your summer program kids compete against each other on the ten event obstacle course that is literally flowing in mud. Include obstacles such as a tarzan swing; barrels and jumps; hay bales; and auto tires. Also have a slide into the mud; basketball shot into a garbage can, while running through the mud; jump a hurdle and land in the mud; crawl through a barrel filled with mud; zigzag run through the mud; balance beam and broad jump. On a separate day invite the public to participate. For an added event, lay out a volleyball court with a foot of mud as the base. The court is rimmed by sandbags.

Memphis Park Commission, 2599 Avery, Memphis, TN 38112

BELLY FLOP AND CANNONBALL CHAMPIONSHIPS

Contestants must weigh at least 250 pounds and are judged on the height of their splash, the amount of water displaced, style, colorfulness of their costume.

SPAGHETTI WRESTLE

A local Italian restaurant might "bite into" this co-sponsorship. Cooked and oiled spaghetti is dumped into children's rubber pools. A balloon is tied onto each wrestler's back. The wrestling begins and when the balloon pops that contestant is out. Winners receive a free dinner for two at the Italian restaurant.

GREAT AMERICAN OUTHOUSE RACE

Different clubs, organizations, businesses and individuals build outhouses on wheels and race them (with an occupant inside) on Main Street. This can be scheduled during an existing festival or as an event in itself.

RECREATOR'S
TOOL BOX

PROGRAM CHECKLIST

EVENT _____

	DATE	COMPLETED
Review: A. Previous Evaluation Forms	———	———
B. Previous Detail Sheets	———	———
C. Previous Financial Statement	———	———
Complete Detail Sheet	———	———
Establish Dates For:		
A. Organizational Staff Meeting	———	———
B. Registration Period	———	———
C. Start Of Event/Program	———	———
D. End Of Event/Program	———	———
Finalize Sponsors	———	———
Prepare/Update Registration Forms/Brochures	———	———
Prepare PSA's Information, Dates to Office Staff	———	———
Inspect Facilities, Work Orders to Parks & Grounds	———	———
Complete Applicable Permits	———	———
Order Supplies	———	———
Select and Train Staff	———	———
Prepare For Organizational/Staff Meeting	———	———
Collect Equipment Supplies	———	———
Write Follow Up Communication	———	———
Prepare Evaluation/Financial Report	———	———

EVENT RESPONSIBILITY PUNCH SHEET

EVENT————————————————

			Parks & Recreation	Comments
Event Permit				
Police				
EMS				
Tents				
Maps				
Start/Finsih Supports				
Finish Supports				
Finish Procedures				
Stop Watches				
Finish Clock				
Finish Cards				
Results				
Tables & Chairs				
Water Stations				
Water Tank				
Personnel for Water				
Fruit				
Spray Stations				
Spotters				
Traffic Control				
Barricades				
Parking Signs				
Van (Results)				
Trash Cans & Pick-Up				
Radios				
Paper Weights				
Bleachers				
PA System				
Portalet				
Concession Trailer				
Sweep Course				
Hay Bales				
Course Lay-Out				
Mlle Splits				
Course Monitors				
Bike For Lead				
Starting Pistol				
Master of Ceremonies				
Packet Gift				
Race Packets				
Signs for Race				
Money Bag & Change				

EVENT_____

		Parks & Recreation	Comments
Photography			
Prizes			
Straight Pins			
TV Coverage			
Advertising			
Entry Forms			
Race Numbers			
Race Day Entry			
Start/Finish Banner			
Results to Media			

MATERIALS CHECKLIST

EVENT _____

	NEED	PACKED		NEED	PACKED
Bottle Opener	___	___	Tape	___	___
Camera	___	___	Duct	___	___
Film	___	___	Masking	___	___
Cassette Tape	___	___	Scotch	___	___
Certificates	___	___	Trash Bags	___	___
Clip Boards	___	___	T-Shirts	___	___
Cups	___	___	Trophies	___	___
Cutting Board	___	___	Walkie Talkies	___	___
Department Banner	___	___	Water Containers	___	___
Direction Signs	___	___	Wire	___	___
Eating Utensils	___	___	___	___	___
Extension Cord	___	___	___	___	___
Flagging	___	___	___	___	___
Flyers	___	___	___	___	___
Hammer	___	___	___	___	___
Hole Punch	___	___	___	___	___
Tape Deck	___	___	___	___	___
Knife	___	___	___	___	___
Legal Pad	___	___	___	___	___
Markers	___	___	___	___	___
Medals	___	___	___	___	___
Megaphone	___	___	___	___	___
Money Box	___	___	___	___	___
Change	___	___	___	___	___
Napkins	___	___	___	___	___
Nails	___	___	___	___	___
PA System	___	___	___	___	___
Paper Weights	___	___	___	___	___
Pencils	___	___	___	___	___
Plates	___	___	___	___	___
Poster Board	___	___	___	___	___
Registration Forms	___	___	___	___	___
Completed Forms	___	___	___	___	___
Rope	___	___	___	___	___
Sandwich Board	___	___	___	___	___
Staple Gun	___	___	___	___	___
Staples	___	___	___	___	___

PROGRAM EVALUATION FORM

PROGRAM_____

DATE & TIME_____

LOCATION_____

AGES INVOLVED_____

STAFF_____
_____

VOLUNTEERS_____

PROGRAM DESCRIPTION _____
_____
_____

PROGRAM GOALS_____
_____
_____

STRONG POINTS_____
_____
_____

TO BE IMPROVED_____
_____
_____

SHOULD PROGRAM BE REPEATED? WHY?_____
_____
_____

SUGGESTIONS FOR NEXT TIME _____
_____
_____

FAVORITE ACTIVITY_____
_____

EXPENDITURES_____
_____

REVENUE_____
_____

SPECIAL MEDIA COVERAGE RECEIVED (DATES, PLACES, PHOTOGRAPHER'S NAME) _____
_____

OVERALL IMPRESSION AND COMMENTS _____
_____
_____

50 GREAT WAYS TO PROMOTE YOUR DEPARTMENT AND EVENTS

1. **NEWSPAPER PUBLICITY.** Keep the phone number of your city editor handy.
2. **RADIO.** Get to know your local radio personalities, disc jockeys. Have them give away tickets to your events.
3. **TELEVISION.** Contact producers of local shows, news broadcasts.
4. **DIRECT MAIL.** Keep in touch with potential patrons through mailings.
5. **BILLBOARDS.** Use painted or poster boards for full-time exposure.
6. **BROCHURES.** Rely on professional help to make them look good.
7. **BUMPER STICKERS.** A good investment - but don't waste them.
8. **DECALS-STICKERS-PATCHES.** Teenagers, in particular, like this identification.
9. **CO-OPERATIVE ADVERTISING.** Share cost with other operators.
10. **EXCHANGE ADVERTISING.** Swap what you have for mention in store ads.
11. **SIGNS.** Use the best to give your operation appeal and class.
12. **DEPARTMENT STORE TIE-INS.** Swap for window and ad space.
13. **RECREATION DIRECTOR.** Check to see how you can help each other.
14. **PERSONALITIES.** Get area, sectional, national figures to appear in person.
15. **REMOTE BROADCASTS.** Radio and TV programs direct from your location.
16. **PHOTO CONTESTS.** Give prizes for best photos taken on the premises.
17. **SERVICE FIRM TIE-INS.** Dairies, diaper firms, gas stations, etc.
18. **CHAMBER OF COMMERCE.** If they know about you they can plug you.
19. **PUBLIC APPRECIATION DAY.** Show your patrons how much you like them.
20. **FILM OR SLIDES.** Prepare for showing to school, church, club groups.
21. **WHAT'S DIFFERENT?** Check for unusual story items; call your newspaper.
22. **IDENTIFY ALL SOUVENIRS.** Good reminders for your customers.
23. **POSTCARDS.** Either sell or give away these colorful souvenirs.
24. **PHOTO BACKGROUNDS.** Create special areas for picture taking.
25. **SPECIAL CERTIFICATES.** Award them for kiddie proficiency.
26. **PERSONALIZE.** Everything the customer uses - paper cups, plates, etc.
27. **GOOFY, LOW COST OR NO-COST PRIZES.** Give 'em away for laughs.
28. **STATE DIRECTORIES.**
29. **TRANSPORTATION ADVERTISING.** Use low-cost taxi, bus, subway ads.
30. **LISTINGS.** Be sure your operation appears in city, county, state directories.
31. **YELLOW PAGES.** Use a listing in your telephone book classified section.
32. **GIVE TALKS.** Appear before civic, fraternal groups.
33. **CATCHY SLOGAN.** Adopt an easy-to-repeat identification.
34. **GREETER-HOST.** Appoint one in an official capacity.
35. **REGULAR BULLETIN.** A mimeographed newsletter will sustain interest.
36. **EXHIBIT.** At local home, sports and trade shows.
37. **CHARITY TIE-INS.** Associate with any and all worthy causes.
38. **COMBAT DELINQUENCY.** Get mayor's proclamation, civic and police support.
39. **FIREWORKS.** Give the public a "safe and sane" display.
40. **IMPRINTS.** Sell or award personalized t-shirts, caps, etc.
41. **GOOD NEIGHBOR.** Lend your equipment or services to worthy local events.
42. **ATTRACTIVE FLOAT.** Keep the base, or a plan, for participation in parades.
43. **OLD FOLKS.** Don't forget them - have a contest for grandmas or grandpas.

It's A Snap!

44. **CHRISTMAS AD.** Even if you're closed, greet your customers.

45. **LUCKY COUPONS.** Put them in popcorn boxes, other packaged confections.

46. **LITTLE LEAGUE TEAM.** Sponsor one for good community relations

47. **NAME CONTESTS.** Hold them for new attractions.

48. **COLORING CONTESTS.** Winning kids get free passes.

49. **MEET YOUR HERO.** A sports celebrity in person to sign autographs.

50. **LOOK AHEAD.** Give planned new features a big build-up.

PROMOTIONAL IDEAS AND GIMMICKS

Following is a list of some techniques of advertising and promoting programs and events.

A **LOGO** is a trademark or symbol that is constantly associated with a product or an event or series. These should be used consistently on all visual publicity materials.

Development of **MAILING LISTS** built around different subject areas, i.e. interest in sports programs, arts and crafts, after school programs, summer programs, senior's events, etc. will enable you to target specific groups that will be interested in upcoming events. Send them brochures, entry forms, etc.

Record companies will supply biographies and **RECORDS** of the groups or individuals who will be performing at your event. Play the records, tapes, or CD's at your center, or have the local radio and TV stations use them in promoting the event.

Agencies will supply **PRESS KITS** which may include photos and reviews of the group performing. You can use these when approaching the local newspaper or campus newspapers.

Arrange **RADIO PREVIEWS**, either through interviews or a recording of the group aired on local radio and TV stations one to two weeks prior to the event. Replay many times during the week of the event.

Use **TEASERS** in the form of ads, posters, buttons, pins, radio announcements, newspaper ads, etc. to begin a program publicity campaign.

During some other program at your center, **PREVIEW** a film or play a record of the group that will be playing at your event.

Use **BUTTONS** to advertise a program or series. Sell buttons as tickets and admission to an event. Sell weeks in advance to expose event.

BUMPER STICKERS - Create all sorts; you name it.

SCREEN T-SHIRTS - Sell t-shirts, or wear them to advertise an upcoming event.

CREATE A CORE GROUP OF INDIVIDUALS who have extensive information about the project who will then speak to various groups. The immediate one-to-one contact in which questions can be answered is more time consuming, but often the most productive, especially in the case of recruiting for volunteers.

Print up a colorful **BOOKMARK** with advertising about a service available or a series of classes or road races, etc.

Use large surplus **WEATHER BALLOONS** with advertising on them to create interest in an area of a display.

A college or high school **CAMPUS NEWSPAPER** can be one of your best forms of advertising, both from ads that you purchase and also feature coverage about upcoming attractions. It is important to develop a good working relationship with the newspaper staff. Possible incentives may be in the form of a few well placed free tickets for events you would like reviewed.

Ask the local **EDUCATIONAL TV** or **CABLE TV** station to run a preview show of upcoming events.

Hang well made **BANNERS** or strings of **BALLOONS** for big events.

Put large signs and **BANNERS** on **AUTOMOBILES** and park them in prime locations in parking lots.

Involve theatre arts **STUDENTS** by having them pass out information about an event.

Paste contact **PAPER FOOTPRINTS** on sidewalks with information on the specific event or place the footprints in such a manner that they lead to the event area, itself. You could have these slogans printed up as you would bumper stickers, and stick them on the sidewalks.

Utilize areas on **CONSTRUCTION FENCES** for posters or have a "paint-in."

Arrange to have **PUBLIC SERVICE ANNOUNCEMENTS** over local radio and TV stations. Public media must provide this service by law.

Realizing that some posters will become wall decorations, make the rounds several times before the event to hang and **REHANG POSTERS**.

LUCKY TICKET DRAWING at major athletic events; give out tickets to future events or activities, in conjunction with half time activities.

Use **SANDWICH BOARDS** to publicize events. Hang them on people and have them walk around events that take place prior to the event you are promoting.

To publicize a drug information program, obtain **EMPTY DRUG CAPSULES** and stuff them with anti-drug messages and slogans and spread them around school campuses.

Pass out **BROCHURES** or **FLYERS** on cars. Some malls, etc. may have regulations against this; check first before distributing.

Give out **FREE TICKETS** to up-coming events to the first "so- many" participants who show up at an event.

Make the event publicity a **LIVING THING** that carries through the theme of the event, i.e., people in clown costumes parading through an event or mall prior to a carnival.

Be sure to **BROCHURE ALL LINES**. Registration line, cafeteria line, theatre ticket lines, and lines to get into lines.

Start a large **SCRAPBOOK** of posters. This will enable future employees or committees to see examples of poster layouts and the quality of posters that have been used in the past.

Have special **FORTUNE COOKIES** made up with information reguarding upcoming events.

JOHN LETTERS. Create a weekly or monthly newsletter containing information about upcoming events and place on the back of restroom doors throughout the city. Large office buildings and restaurants are great distribution places.

Give away **POSTERS** or **BOOK COVERS** in advance of an event or series of events. Do this in place of calendars.

POCKET CALENDAR - Have a calendar of upcoming events printed on cards.

Set up a **CALL-IN TAPED CALENDAR.** Publicize a phone number that could be called night or day containing a recorded message of current events, times, where to get tickets, etc. The tape is changed as events change and provides a great service to the community. Call it the Leisure Line.

INSERTS in campus newspapers and local newspapers reach thousands for a very low cost per thousand.

DOOR KNOB CARDS - Take a tip from the "do not disturb" signs used by motels and have your message printed on a card of this type. Take them to the residence halls on the college campus and hang one on each door knob.

DROPS ADS. Contact can be made with newspaper advertisers for a "drop ad." This a very small amount of copy, no more than five or six words, dropped into an advertisers ad, to remind the readership. The copy might be placed inside a circle, square, or whatever, to attract attention and set it apart from the rest of the ad.

COMMUNITY RESOURCES

Call on various agencies and businesses, such as these, to assist you with your programming.

ART COUNCILS -
Art fairs, concerts in the park, theatrical productions/plays.

BAKERIES -
Cake decorating classes, bread and coffee cake making classes/demonstrations.

BANKS -
Money management seminars, balancing a checkbook workshop, loan options, charge cards, computer services, facilities/meeting rooms for classes, payroll.

BUS COMPANIES -
Transportation for day camp field trips, senior citizen trips.

CAR DEALERS -
How to buy a new/used car, simple body repair workshops, powder puff mechanics class.

CHURCHES -
Facilities/meeting rooms, retreat centers, gymnasiums, babysitting.

COLLEGES AND UNIVERSITIES -
Faculty loan and exchange to instruct various programs, consulting, interns, career development, facilities, programs/seminars, sports/theatrical events.

CORPORATIONS -
Advertising, team and award sponsorship. Fast Food Restaurants - syrup concentrate, napkins, paper plates, free coupons, large drink dispensers, food for events, birthday parties.

FIRE DEPARTMENTS -
Fire protection facts, babysitting clinics, basic first aid, CPR clinics and certification.

FLORISTS -
Flower arranging classes, dried flower arrangements, plant care, corsages for special events/dances.

FURNITURE STORES -
Furniture repair, interior decoration techniques, furniture refinishing workshops.

GAS STATIONS -
Clinics on how to change a tire/jump a car, emergency services that are available, basic car maintenance classes, how to pump gas/check the oil.

GROCERY STORES -
Food for special events/luncheons, discount prices on day-old items, publicity of events.

HARDWARE STORES -
Workshops on insulating your home, lawn and garden care, simple home repair, and paneling a room.

HEALTH FOOD STORES -
Seminars on natural nutrition, using herbs and spices properly, cooking with natural foods, and natural vitamins.

HOSPITALS -
Consulting, first aid supplies, coordination of programs, health related seminars, fitness court grants.

JAYCEES -
Additional staff support for haunted house, Easter egg hunt, bike rodeo.

LABOR UNIONS -
Team sponsors, construction, planning/design consultants, surplus tools and equipment.

LIBRARIES -
Story hours, free movies/album loans, publicity, resource people.

PAINT STORES -
Workshops on hanging wallpaper and interior and exterior painting, seminar on low cost decorating ideas, supplies for special events.

PERSONNEL DEPARTMENTS -
Assist with proper interviewing techniques and developing job descriptions/applications.

POLICE DEPARTMENTS -

Bike rodeos that include bike saftey and bike registration, rape prevention seminars, preschool "stranger danger" program.

PRINTERS -

Assist with brochure/flyer layout and design, inexpensive printing methods, scrap paper for arts and crafts programs.

PUBLIC RELATIONS FIRMS -

Flyer design, assist with a marketing plan, seminars for staff training, consulting.

REAL ESTATE AGENCIES -

Trends and current statistics on your community, technical assistance, rental space available in town for haunted house, long range plans, "for sale" sign frames for special event advertising.

RED CROSS -

CPR for staff, program co-sponsorship, movie rentals, instructors.

SCHOOLS -

Facilities, equipment, staff/teachers to instruct recreation department classes, student teachers.

SENIOR CITIZENS/CLUBS -

Babysitters, instructors, arts and crafts for bazaars, publicity, bake sales, fund raising.

GREAT SPECIAL EVENTS AND ACTIVITIES, PART II ????

If you would like to have an event(s) included in GREAT SPECIAL EVENTS AND ACTIVITIES, PART II, please complete the following form and send to: Venture Publishing, Inc., 1999 Cato Avenue, State College, PA 16801.

EVENT:

DESCRIPTION:

RELATED ACTIVITIES:

MATERIALS:

POSSIBLE RESOURCES:

A) FOR ASSISTANCE

B) FOR PARTICIPATION

CREATIVE PROMOTIONS:

JUDGING CATEGORIES:

• •

Name _____

Department _____

Address _____

City _____ State _____ Zip _____

Phone (work) _____ (home) _____